D0350640

Martinez Kiwanis

donates this book in the name of
Dick Blair, CC Reg. Health Foundation
in appreciation for the
program presentation made to
the Kiwanis Club in 2008

What's Your Body Telling You?

Listening to Your Body's Signals to Stop Anxiety, Erase Self-Doubt, and Achieve True Wellness

STEVE SISGOLD
FOREWORD BY GAY HENDRICKS

New York   Chicago   San Francisco   Lisbon   London   Madrid   Mexico City
Milan   New Delhi   San Juan   Seoul   Singapore   Sydney   Toronto

Library of Congress Cataloging-in-Publication Data

Sisgold, Steve.
    What's your body telling you? : listening to your body's signals to stop anxiety,
    erase self-doubt, and achieve true wellness / Steve Sisgold.
        p.   cm.
    ISBN 978-0-07-162457-2 (alk. paper)
    1. Body, Human (Philosophy).   2. Body image.   3. Personality.
    4. Decision making.   I. Title.

    B105.B64S59   2009
    158.1—dc22   2008047898

1 2 3 4 5 6 7 8 9 10 11 12 13 14 15 16 17 18 19 20 21 22 DOC/DOC 0 9

ISBN   978-0-07-162457-2
MHID   0-07-162457-0

McGraw-Hill books are available at special quantity discounts to use as premiums and
sales promotions or for use in corporate training programs. To contact a representative,
please visit the Contact Us pages at www.mhprofessional.com.

This book is printed on acid-free paper.

To Morris and Tillye Sisgold

*I am forever blessed and grateful for your
love, inspiration, and acceptance.*

CONTENTS

CHAPTER

≋ 3 ≋

Whole-Body Inquiry 25

Four Tools to Activate the Brilliance of Your Body 26
How High Is Your BQ? 28
The Library of Your Cells: Your Body Biography 30
Each Body Has a Unique Signature: Your
Body Personality 41
Your Most Decisive Communication: Your
Body Billboard 48

CHAPTER

≋ 4 ≋

Ready—SET—Go! 51

Access the Now with SET (Self-Evident Truth) 52
Living in the Beam 57
How You Can Use SET to Stop the Spin 58
Your Body as a Thought Monitor 61
Catching the Beat 63
Upward, Downward, and Wayward Thoughts 65

CHAPTER

≋ 5 ≋

Viral Beliefs 69

Your Reality-Making Blueprint 71
Who Makes This Stuff Up? 73
Paper Tigers 76
The Enthusiasm Thief 78
Deeper to Diamonds 86
Embody the Antidote 89

CHAPTER

·························· ≩ 12 ≨ ··························

A Day in the Life of Whole-Body Consciousness 205

The India Odyssey 207
What Am I Doing Here? 208
Cow Consciousness 209
An Impromptu Meeting with the Dalai Lama 210
Udder Happiness 212

FOREWORD
Gay Hendricks, Ph.D.

THIS IS A timeless book on a timeless subject: the art of creating what you most want and enjoying what you have. By timeless, I mean that you could pick it up ten years or a hundred years from now and its wisdom would be just as relevant as it is today. It also brings a uniquely balanced approach to a field that sees a fair amount of extremist philosophies. Most of the books on manifestation I've read are too cognitive, leaving the body out of the process, or too metaphysical, missing the specific action steps that ground the concept in clear, physical reality. Steve Sisgold shows how to most effectively use the full range of human potential: physical, emotional, mental, and spiritual.

I have had the great pleasure of knowing Steve for many years. I first heard of him through friends, who raved about his successful work in coaching authors and musicians I knew or admired. Later, my wife, Kathlyn, and I engaged his services to help us create the organization and career focus that we needed. I look back on that decision as one of the watershed moments of my life. Although we were already quite successful, there were many goals we would have liked to achieve that seemed impossible and outside our reach. Within a short time, using the information and practices Steve offered, we manifested them all, including appearing on "The Oprah Winfrey Show" twice. This is the power of Steve's gift: showing how to translate your dreams into clear action steps, all grounded in love, balance, and purpose.

One of the things I most admire about Steve is that he is a man of many talents. He is equally at home giving a heartfelt motivational speech, strumming a tune he's written on his guitar, and cheering at a Warriors basketball game with his son. He knows how to make his own dreams into reality, in every area of his life, and he has inspired thousands of others to do the same.

I urge you to make use of this book in your work, leisure, personal relationships, and everywhere else, even if you are already successful. There's a natural longing in all of us to make full use of our inherent gifts. Steve recognizes this, and he has developed powerful—and powerfully simple—techniques for drawing out your gifts.

May this fine work assist you on your path to a life of passion and purpose.

ACKNOWLEDGMENTS

I AM BLESSED TO have met so many good people through my work over the years. To all of you, I am honored by your willingness to tune in to your body's intelligence with me. It's you who have inspired me to write this.

When my agent took this book to market I had one wish: to sign with a publisher who understood and appreciated the importance of my message. I found that in the McGraw-Hill team—especially in my dream editor there, Emily Carleton. She is the savvy, caring, skilled team player who positioned my book to be its best for you.

I also applaud Gayathri Vinay in Marketing and Kenya Henderson in Publicity for their top-notch collaborative efforts.

I thank my friends and agents Michael Ebeling and Kristina Holmes for helping me connect with the best publisher for this book. You nailed it.

Big bravo to Geralyn Gendreau, who for three solid months helped me express my voice in the book in the best way possible. You taught me how 2 = 10, and I will be forever grateful for that lesson as well as your insights and out-of-the-box editing skills.

And special thanks to Doug Childers for your great editing and suggestions for my book proposal and your steady, consistent belief in my book.

Thank you Gay Hendricks for joining me on one of the most transformational journeys of my life, in Germany and Poland. It is forever inscribed in my cells and this book. I look forward to more aha moments shared together.

Special gratitude to Will Wilkinson, Clifton Mack, Vinit Allen, Craig Bolt, and Joe Wolf for enhancing this book. Thank you all.

To my son, Jesse Sisgold, I thank you for teaching me about unconditional love and for being my best friend for over thirty-three years. Life has taken on so much more meaning since your birth. You make me proud every day. Now I get to thank you professionally, too, for your inspiration, insights, and writing and for being my advisor, word by word, chapter by chapter.

To my partner, Amanda Snow, I am a very blessed man to have met you while writing this book. Your intuition, expanded perspectives, and advice have been such special gifts to me and to this book. Having your love, nurturing, and encouragement makes all the difference in the world to me at this exciting time of my life. I am so glad to be going on this journey side by side with you.

INTRODUCTION

What Is Whole-Body Consciousness?

You Have an Ally

YOUR ALLY holds a map to your destiny, your deepest desires and dreams.

Your ally is your best friend and counselor—the ultimate success coach.

Your ally supplies you with key insights and information whenever you need it.

Your ally monitors your health, relationships, and finances with a clear eye.

Your ally shows you the deepest truth in any moment in the most direct and simple way.

Your ally can clear your mind in an instant, and erase fear and doubt in a heartbeat.

Your ally is on call and in your corner twenty-four hours a day.

Your ally is your brilliant body!

A Five-Star Thrill Ride

An amazing and unpredictable adventure began when you were conceived. From that very moment, your innate intelligence has steered you through a nonstop stream of sensations, feelings, thoughts, and impressions that make up the five-star thrill ride called life. Sometimes this kaleidoscopic stream of stimuli makes sense to you, and you navigate it easily. Other times a wave of feeling or sudden event comes your way and sweeps you off course. Either way, *everything that happens to you is registered in your body,* literally etched in your cells and your consciousness. Your body is infinitely complex and fantastically creative. It has a huge capacity to receive, process, and integrate highly energized information—even when stuck in difficult circumstances or painful experiences. Constantly scanning both within and without, your body sorts and prioritizes all that information so you can function effectively. Regardless of where your attention might wander, your body knows all it needs to know.

I call your body "brilliant" because of its sophisticated somatic intelligence, its boundless memory, and its unique, intuitive guidance system. All your experience and knowledge, your pain and joy, your forgotten secrets and your deepest desires are recorded there. As a result, your body has its own intelligence—a natural grasp of the deeper truths your mind alone cannot comprehend. The best move you can make, in many situations, is to get out of your head and into your body.

Your body speaks to you directly in the language of sensations, most notably *primary feelings,* such as tension, temperature changes, butterflies, nausea, headaches, changes in breath—even a rush of elation! Unfortunately, primary feelings are oftentimes lost in a wash of secondary emotion that is triggered by an unresolved past—both your individual past and humanity's collective past.

For over twenty years, I've enjoyed teaching clients and seminar participants how to get out of their heads and access their internal guidance system. People are consistently amazed to discover that they can truly rely on the body's deep authority as a navigator. The insights and methodology contained in this book have been tested over and over, with great results. Many people experience remarkable personal and professional breakthroughs once they tap into their body-based intelligence. My clients have found all kinds of success—including Grammy awards, world championship poker titles, and best-selling books. Others have used whole-body consciousness to overcome personal tragedy, break free of crippling addictions, start a new career, or attract a loving life partner.

This book is designed to catalyze a key alliance—the one between your mind and body—and free you from the straight-jacket of outdated thinking that keeps you treating them as two separate entities. As you read, page by page, you will feel your body come alive. You will begin to appreciate it for its true brilliance, even if you have concerns about how it may look or perform for you right now.

People find something priceless and unexpected when they tap into the natural brilliance of their bodies. This book is full of their stories—real-life accounts that demonstrate the power that lies—usually dormant—within each of us. You can activate this power and use it to heal, to grow, to awaken, and to create the life of your dreams. In the pages that follow, you will learn how to hear and understand your body's primal communications. By the end, you will be able to shift into whole body consciousness at will, and *just know* what the next right move is for you. You will learn to communicate with greater effectiveness and clarity, and you will be able to identify, release, and change the subconscious beliefs that sabotage your happiness. You will learn how to find and heal old traumas and painful emotions that may be stored in your body. In essence, you will reclaim your natural ability to determine what it is you truly desire and consistently achieve the outcomes that are aligned with your higher purpose.

This work is the culmination of a prolonged and systematic study of body language, somatic intelligence, psychology, and spirituality as they relate to human health, well-being, and success. My investigation has taken me around the world to study and practice various spiritual teachings and methods, both ancient and modern.

Everywhere I go, across countries, cultures, and stations of life, I have observed this basic truth: whole-body consciousness makes you more intelligent—better able to discern what you want and what's in your way, and become unstoppable. On a micro level, in your personal life, WBC gives you the confidence you need to face family, economic, health, or other issues head-on. On a macro level, just imagine the positive influence you can have on the world if you access the mind in your heart and the mind in your gut—and use these in harmony with the mind in your skull.

This book is designed to walk you through a body-mind-heart integration process that attunes and harmonizes your entire being. Read, reflect, and jump into the exercises, and you will develop a closer relationship with your body, an expanded sense of purpose, greater faith in humanity, and an increased capacity for love and happiness that emanates from your true core. I applaud and thank you for joining me in this journey of self-discovery. Let's begin!

CHAPTER

I

Your Body Rocks

The body is a device to calculate the astronomy of the spirit;
look through that astrolabe and become oceanic.

—RUMI

.... ⋲ Baltimore, Maryland, 1961 ⋲ ....

SITTING IN MY usual seat at the family dinner table, I feel a surge of energy coursing through my twelve-year-old body. My father has just put his lifelong dream into words: "Midget Grocery has one of its stores up for sale; I want to buy it and run my own business." His excitement is tangible; the air feels electrified. My mother, who was not privy to his plan before this announcement, looks a bit stunned. After a pause, she begins to marshal a series of practical arguments for why he should forget the whole idea.

"What? And give up your management position with an established grocery chain?"

My father has always had a predictable schedule and a dependable salary that provides quite a bit of security for our family. My mom's reasons are solid, and her arguments perfectly sensible. The risk to our family's financial picture is too great—end of story. Pass the blintzes, please.

1

I try my darnedest to keep a lid on my feelings. Thoughts race through my head: *Don't interrupt! . . . You better keep quiet! . . . Mind your own business. . . . What do you know? You're just a kid.* But my body, with heart thumping, will hear nothing of it. A strong sense of certainty washes over me, and I cannot keep quiet. Like the cork on a bottle of bubbly, I pop: *"Dad, get the store! You can do it!"* I look at my mom with soft eyes of apology, but inside I feel like James Brown strutting the one-step and singing, "I feel good."

The morning after my dinner-table outburst, my mom agrees to accompany my dad and take a look at the store, saying, "Why not? We'll see the place, and afterward we'll get a corned beef sandwich."

I'll never be sure how much I influenced her by blurting out my conviction, but five minutes after she walked into the store, my mother changed her tune and supported my father's decision to buy it. One week after my father opened his store, a statewide food strike closed down all the local supermarket chains. People lined up halfway down the block waiting to buy their groceries. This went on for weeks, and many of them became long-term customers. The opening of his first business, Super Discount, was a personal triumph for my dad. He loved working for himself, and my mom leapt at the chance to work as his right hand. He became an overnight success by following his instinct, which was encouraged by mine.

A New Kind of Awareness

The lesson I learned at the dinner table that night was pivotal. It was a marker moment in my life—that flash of conviction searing through my body and compelling me to blurt out, *"You can do it!"* What I didn't understand at the time (and couldn't put into words until much, much later) was that it was my first experience with *whole-body consciousness*—an expanded form of awareness that transcends and expands our rational way of knowing. I literally became a different kind of person than I had been before. Taking the risk required to break with convention and speak aloud what I simply *knew in my body beyond all reason* changed me at a very basic level. A kind of knowledge outside the dominion of rational thought had revealed itself. I would not notice or name this subtle shift for quite some time, and yet the net effect of my outburst was evidenced quickly. My father's work life immediately improved, and our family life took a turn for the better as well.

The Queen of Diamonds

Fast-forward some forty years to another table, where whole-body consciousness is about to yield keen awareness once again. This time the key player is not a wisecracking preteen but a dynamo political strategist. Nancy Todd Tyner has run 196 political campaigns in forty-two states and six countries—and won 98 percent of them.

Nancy first learned to play poker at her family's kitchen table when she was a girl. A resident of Las Vegas, Nancy had watched the World Poker Tour on television but rarely went into the casinos. All that changed in the months that followed the death of her fourteen-year-old son. Hayden had died of cancer, and to keep from going crazy with grief one night, Nancy fled to the noise and lights of the MGM Grand and sat down at a poker table. Surprised at how readily her skill as a political strategist transferred to the competitive atmosphere of tournament poker, she got hooked. The game gave her something to look forward to during her otherwise dismal days of grief. The more Nancy played, the clearer she became about her goal: she wanted to become the first woman to win the male-dominated World Series of Poker tournament. She continued to build her skills and even attended World Poker Tour Boot Camp.

But somewhere along the line, Nancy's confidence began to falter. She found herself distracted by errant thoughts and self-doubt, especially when sitting at the poker table with men. She started to overthink her instincts in an effort to show the men she was no dumb blond, and distracting thoughts arose when she faced female opponents. In an interview on national television, Nancy talked about the type of mental noise that often got in her way: "When I first started playing, someone told me, lose the jewelry, tone it down, and I took it to heart, but when I showed up, I wasn't comfortable." Competitive anxiety from the past would flood Nancy's mind and make it impossible to remain present and alert in the game. This woman, who rarely saw a loss in the cutthroat world of politics, found it difficult to manage her thoughts and feelings when she lost a hand. But Nancy wasn't ready to walk away and felt certain in her gut that if she stuck with it, she could win at this game, too. But she knew she needed help to get the defeatist voices out of her mind.

Nancy called and set up a one-day intensive with me. A quick study, she learned to get out of her head and access whole-body consciousness at will through the same simple steps I've taught thousands of people in my seminars and which you'll read about in the chapters that follow. Nancy learned to recognize when her thinking got caught in what I call a *spin trap*—those dead-end thought loops in which distracted, fear-based thinking makes the natural intelligence of the body impossible to hear. Together we uncovered the fearful beliefs that fed her negative thoughts. I led her through an exercise to discover and embody her larger life purpose, and this clarity shed new light on her zest for poker. What was initially a means to an end—coping with her grief—became a platform from which she now speaks out on cancer education to help parents whose children have been struck with the disease.

With renewed inspiration, Nancy set an initial goal to win the first women's World Poker Tour Championship. The going was tough at first. Nancy had to face down the negative thoughts and beliefs that prompted her to make desperate, losing moves. After going through a host of tournaments, she developed much greater awareness of her internal mechanism as well as the external bodily signals that gave her away. It worked—and fast. Instead of getting eliminated in the first round, she moved up to the final tables several events in a row. With certainty and a new winning edge, she entered the World Poker Tour Ladies Championship.

Nancy's political career had taught her all she needed to know about being the underdog. She knows the long-shot territory better than most. When the two top sponsors, Poker Stars and Full Tilt Poker, declined to back her, she was unfazed. One representative said, "No need to take on another horse," citing the fact that they had all three pros at the table and were certain of a win. As a political strategist, Nancy was regularly cast in the role of David against some Goliath of a campaign. She was amused to find herself on familiar ground.

············   ≣ **Bellagio Hotel, Spring 2008** ≣   ············
The Inaugural WPT Ladies Championship

"The Queen of Diamonds," Nancy Todd Tyner, is head-to-head with "the Brooklyn Bluffer," Vanessa Selbst, the heavy favorite here at the finals table. Vanessa has Nancy on the ropes. Nancy looks down at her dwindling pile of chips and realizes she has slipped into her old pattern of spin-thinking and needs to regroup. She asks for a time-out and takes a break. While alone in the ladies' room, Nancy realigns with her purpose by talking aloud to her son: "Hayden, I didn't come here to lose, and I have no intention of it. I'm not asking for aces and kings, I'm asking you to help me read my opponent. . . . Then I can do this."

Nancy returns to the table and breathes deeply into her body to access whole-body consciousness. She reaches into her bag for her iPod and listens briefly to a digital recording of my voice, reminding her that she can avoid reacting to her opponent by getting out of her head and expanding her awareness. The light goes on—*I can't read my opponent if I'm not reading myself.* She scans her body and notices the tension that has her leaning forward with an anxious look on her face. She sits back, feels her natural winning instinct return, and takes the next hand. She is back in the zone. Her bejeweled fingers sparkle—*bling, bling.* Two, three hours pass as the two women fight for every chip.

At one point, Vanessa looks Nancy in the eye and says, "You know, you should smile more. . . . We're both going to make a lot of money tonight."

"Honestly," Nancy says, "I'm not playing for the money."

That puts an end to distracting chitchat.

Within an hour, Nancy emerged victorious and took home the purse—a $68,640 first prize. The next day, the local media pronounced: "Todd Tyner displayed consummate patience . . . and although rather new to the game compared to lots of the tour pros, she played like an old pro, without getting overwhelmed by the final-table aggression." Nancy smiled into the camera in a postwin interview and summed it up this way: "I am a good poker player because I am attuned to everything that is happening while playing."

Nancy has now set her sights on being the first woman to win the male-dominated World Series of Poker tournament. If I were a betting man, I'd wager a pile of chips that she will!

Higher-Order Thinking

What I was able to impress upon Nancy is the simple fact that we all have a brilliant body, with innate intelligence that will serve as an inner compass—if only we let it. A few simple tools and steady application was all it took for Nancy to actualize whole-body consciousness (WBC). In other words, she practiced getting out of her head and put WBC to the test in the laboratory called *high-stakes poker with a purpose*.

Each of us is dealt our own set of circumstances unique to our personal path through life. At times our circumstances are fairly predictable, even boring. At other times, the squeeze of modern life pushes us outside our comfort zone and onto the steep slope of a new learning curve. And sometimes we are faced with a major upheaval—divorce, the loss of a loved one or our source of income. Major disasters, such as a hurricane or a tsunami, come along, and we are forced into volatile conditions utterly beyond our control. Given that life and the larger world are likely to continue pushing and prodding humanity along in this unpredictable way, we owe it to ourselves, to our families, and to our future to upgrade our internal navigation system.

The information and techniques set forth in the chapters that follow will catalyze your brilliant body and familiarize you with WBC so you become well equipped to steer through life, whether you encounter rough waters or calm seas. Especially helpful in rapidly changing times, this resource allows you to step out of mental spin traps where fear and limitation can take over your thoughts and blind you. With whole-body consciousness, you gain a new edge that lets you to drop the illusion created by spin traps in favor of the kind of higher-order thinking Albert Einstein pointed to when he said, "We can't solve problems by using the same kind of thinking we used when we created them."

Stop Overthinking and Start Living

Problem solving is a crucial skill that forces your mind to work through the obstacles that stand between you and your goals. If you are like most people, however, at times you err on the side of overthinking—getting so lost in your head that you lose perspective. Whole-body consciousness allows you to shift gears, disengage from the hyperrational and often reactionary mind, and tap into your inner knowing that holds the solution to every problem. Shifting to whole-body consciousness and listening to what your body is telling you is that quantum move.

Just as you created your own personal identification number to access your bank account, you can create your own whole-body access code to get into whole-body consciousness. You may use kinesthetic, auditory, or visual cues, or some combination of these. To clarify: Feel your hands holding this book right now—that is a kinesthetic cue. Listen to the birds outside or the sounds inside the room—that is an auditory cue. If you say inwardly, "I've slipped into spin thoughts," that is an auditory-kinesthetic cue, because you both hear that inner voice and feel the vibration in your throat. Go look in a mirror at your own eyes—that is a visual cue. Have fun experimenting with various cues and find out what brings you most fully into your body in the moment. You will get to explore this further in Chapter 4 when you learn the "self-evident truth" technique.

Once you know your access code and can readily tune in to WBC, you can adapt to changing circumstances with greater finesse. For instance, let's say you access WBC while driving to work and discover that your hands are gripping the wheel like there's no tomorrow. You breathe into the tightness of your grip and notice that your neck is all crunched up and that your mind is in a constant loop of worrisome thoughts. With this added awareness, you instantly choose to release the tension in your body, breathe deeply into your lower belly, and practice one of the WBC techniques that you will learn in the chapters that follow. Your grip on the wheel loosens, and your worries begin to fade. What's more, should someone swerve into your lane, you'll have the presence of mind to handle it effortlessly and maintain your cool. The ride to work need not set you up for a long day of headaches and neck pain nor threaten your safe-driver status. As you internalize this new awareness, your whole way of thinking, speaking, acting, and navigating through life will change for the better. Biochemically, you're a new person.

This power to shift your biochemistry into a peak state— what I call *being in the beam*—is now being verified in research studies by leading-edge scientists. With WBC you are fully equipped to live your best life.

Intelligence Is as Intelligence Does

Intelligence has nothing whatsoever to do with thought.
. . . Intelligence comes into being when the mind, the
heart, and the body are really harmonious.

—J. KRISHNAMURTI

The inner workings of the body-mind are under the microscope, as modern-day scientists discover just how powerful and diverse human capabilities are. Science has now demonstrated that the mind and body are one system. Only in our human philosophies were they ever separated. A new wave of mind-body scientists and healers are opening up new possibilities for human development in every area of life. We are learning that our physiology affects our emotions. Emotions affect our thinking. Thoughts affect our emotions, which affect our physiology, which then affects feeling and thinking, and so it goes.

A growing body of new research shows the following: (1) feelings contain as much, if not more, information as thoughts, (2) information is stored in our physical bodies at a cellular level, (3) every thought and feeling creates a physiological effect that is etched into our cells, and (4) this information exerts a profound, yet largely subliminal, influence on our perceptions, behaviors, and experience. As cell biologist Bruce Lipton, Ph.D., explains in his book *The Biology of Belief*, "A human organism is a community of upwards of fifty trillion cells operating in unison and harmony, trying to conform to the requests and demands of that central voice. And it is the central voice that acquires and learns the perceptions that we must deal with throughout our lives."

Deepak Chopra, in his foreword to Candace Pert's book *Molecules of Emotion*, refers to the intelligence that resides throughout our entire body as a *mobile brain*. According to Chopra, Pert shows us that "our biochemical messengers act with intelligence by communicating information, orchestrating a vast complex of conscious and unconscious activities at any one moment. This information transfer takes place over a network, linking all of our systems and organs, engaging all of our molecules of emotion, as the means of communication. What we see is an image of a 'mobile brain'—one that moves throughout our entire body, located in all places at once and not just in the head."

We now have new fields of medicine such as *neurogastroen-terology*, founded by Dr. Michael Gershon, author of *The Second Brain*. Gershon is also the chairman of the department of anatomy and cell biology at Columbia, where he focuses on interactions of the central nervous system with the so-called brain-gut axis. Another relatively new field in medicine is *neurocardiology*, which views the heart as an intelligent organ and studies its interactions with both the peripheral nervous system and the central nervous system.

Mind and body have always been one whole and complete system. This is the interdependence that prompted me to challenge my mother's reasonable fears at the dinner table that night long ago. It is also what gave Nancy the certainty to navigate the uncharted waters at the Bellagio Hotel.

Unfortunately, many of us learned to repress our inner knowing when we were told not to speak up at the dinner table. Or we ignored the exquisite direction of the body's navigation system and have difficulty finding our winning edge because we get caught up in spin thoughts just as Nancy did before she tapped into WBC. Let's take a look at how and why this happens and close the gap in awareness—for your body's brilliance, and what it has to tell you, is little more than a breath away.

≡ 2 ≡

Living in Spin

Now it appears to me that almost any man may like the spider
spin from his own inwards his own airy citadel.

—JOHN KEATS, from a letter to John Hamilton Reynolds

I AM A TOTAL optimist and prefer not to focus on doom and gloom, and yet I cannot ignore the obvious reality. We live in a time of great confusion. People's minds have been infected by spin—a contagion of half-truths, fearful fictions, and blatant deceit. No profession, no religion, no society is immune. Experts and charlatans alike step up to dazzle the hopeful. Spin-doctored illusions show up on every front. This virus of falseness has spread to all corners of the globe. No one, it seems, is spared the plague of spin.

Politicians, merchants, our most cherished institutions— all are infected with the spin virus. The media feeds on spin and propagates it until lies and half-truths become synonymous with facts in people's minds. Truth has become passé, unpopular, even taboo. Human values have been seriously distorted and, in some situations, completely lost. Consumed by a bizarre, insatiable appetite for more, people have become obsessed with winning, profiting, hiding, surviving, and getting their way no matter the cost. Language itself has become infected with spin. Words have been turned into shields that make it possible for people to avoid feeling, to hide the truth, and to manipulate one another at every turn. People take sides and stake out their battlegrounds using words as weapons to cover up greedy, self-serving, power-hungry agendas. True power and a confident, regal bearing are rarely seen. We have lost faith in many of our leaders and in each other.

A client recently e-mailed me something she read on the Internet that sheds sarcastic and yet oddly inarguable light on our current milieu: "Generally the best way to tell if a politician is lying is to check if his or her mouth is moving. If the jaw is moving up and down and words are coming out of it, chances are what you are hearing is a deception."

The problem is not limited to politicians, of course. Businesspeople, CEOs, clergymen, movie stars, teachers, diplomats—the list gets exhausting—have raised our ire for their lack of trustworthy character. The expense is tremendous, when deceptions lead to oil spills, glacial meltdown, soaring energy bills, crumbling levies in hurricane country, or mortgage foreclosures for an entire swath of the population. At a micro level, the emotional cost is impossible to measure when husbands, wives, parents, and children get caught up in undeclared spin wars that tear the fabric of family to shreds. Worst of all, we've lost faith in ourselves. Look at the state of our inner lives. Antidepressant use is on the rise, and self-medication through substance use and abuse is still our favorite Band-Aid solution.

If we look at these symptoms and fail to address the underlying problem, our effectiveness will be limited. Why keep putting out fires when evolution is calling us to rise from the ashes? If we are to become like the phoenix, we must cut to the root of the problem and look squarely at this epidemic of fearful thinking, falsehoods, selfish motivations, and shortsighted goals that has infected the human mind with a disingenuous way of being. What Eckhart Tolle calls "the ego" in his bestselling book *A New Earth* is a cultural as well as a personal phenomenon. At the macro level, distortions of egotistic small-mindedness collect and accumulate until we can barely discern what is real.

Spindoctrination: How Your Body's Brilliance Gets Scrambled

It's important to understand how we got here, in the context of our collective evolution. Author Geralyn Gendreau, the founder of the Alliance for Conscious Evolution, recently explained it this way on her blog (August 26, 2008):

> The human mind evolved the ability to deceive another as a means of survival. Early humans used their unique forebrain with its ability to plan and strategize to outwit prey and avoid predators. We then evolved the ability to read a lie; a specific portion of the brain is hard wired to this function. In response to this development, we developed an even higher-order function: *the ability to lie to ourselves.* This uniquely human ability allows us to present an honest face when we are being less than truthful. Once again, the complex human brain devises a survival strategy that allows us to outwit the one we want to deceive—but at what cost? The cost may not be evident in the short run—after all, we closed the deal, or won the settlement, or pulled the wool over a rival's eyes—but in the long run, such deceptions have a tremendous cost. Personal integrity is lost, self esteem is sacrificed, and basic trust is tossed out the window. In time, we lose contact with the truth and are lost in deceptions that have little bearing on what is real in the here and now.

Is it any wonder, then, that we so often encounter a confusing muddle of crosscurrents that bump us off course? I call this *spindoctrination*.

As infants, we live naturally in a state of whole-body consciousness; this was your primary state for the first few years of life. Vitality, curiosity, and passionate enthusiasm literally poured through your body as pure awareness. Whole-body consciousness guided your development with a sure hand as you expanded your awareness moment by moment. Your sophisticated somatic and sensory intelligence—what I call "BQ" for "body intelligence"—was instinctively and masterfully put to good use. In time, however, that unfettered awareness was compelled to narrow its focus. As you grew older, your cognitive awareness began to develop. You learned to rely less and less on body intelligence once your mental intelligence kicked in.

In a culture that places greater value on thinking than feeling and emphasizes reason over gut-knowing, BQ is suppressed or simply goes dormant. Child rearing, socialization, and education in every stage of our lives overlooks or overtly discourages the development of BQ. Let's look at an example of how this happens and what we become as a result.

Robert came for a session because he felt paralyzed by life; he simply could not trust himself to make good decisions. After years of making tentative career and investment moves that failed and choosing incompatible mates, Robert lost confidence in his decision-making power altogether—so much so that that he couldn't even trust himself to know what to order off a menu.

I led him into whole-body consciousness, and he quickly recalled a time in his childhood when he had skinned his knee on the playground. He clearly remembered crying out in pain and being told by the school nurse, "Now, Robert, that doesn't really hurt." Confused by this, Robert stopped crying. The nurse's authority caused him to override his own body-based knowledge. Sound familiar? Robert reported a similar incident that is all too common: He had started to feel warm while riding in a car and took off his sweater. His mom said, "You're not hot," and insisted he put his sweater back on. The whole way to school, he was sweating bullets. Too young to rebel or even question his mother's authority, Robert simply waited it out in a dissociated trance. This set up a pattern wherein Robert could neither register nor trust signals coming from his body. He began to shut down the intricate guidance system that his brilliant body offered to help navigate everyday choices.

Robert is not alone. Many of us have been similarly trained to ignore our inbuilt biofeedback system. Parents, teachers, and role models trained us to disconnect from our feelings and somatic intelligence in order to fit in with and please others. When a child expresses physical or emotional discomfort and is repeatedly met with frustration or disapproval, he or she soon learns that it isn't safe or acceptable to *feel*. The child gets the message, loud and clear—*your body isn't reliable*—and begins to adapt and conform to misguided demands and expectations. The cost to the child is tremendous; both spontaneous self-expression and the simple joy of being are rapidly being lost.

Life Is Not an Out-of-Body Experience

From the moment we begin school we are trained to look outward rather than inward, to focus on facts and practical problems in the external world, to be goal oriented. Virtually nothing in Western education encourages us to reflect on ourselves, our inner lives and motives.

—DANAH ZOHAR AND DR. IAN MARSHALL,
SQ: Connecting with Our Spiritual Intelligence

Most of us never learned about body wisdom, body intelligence, or body awareness in school. "Sit still and be quiet" was the rule of the day, and woe to the kid who was unable to conform. What if children were taught how to manage their energy with correct breathing rather than be commanded day after day to do something as unnatural as sit still? By high school age, young people can readily learn basic awareness practices or exercises for relaxation and stress reduction. In the best scenarios, children get involved in sports, but many merely go through the motions of a physical education class and barely learn how to do push-ups and sit-ups. Our educational system is so outwardly focused and places so little emphasis on self-awareness that most of us are led away from the body and become desensitized to feelings. Our natural instincts begin to atrophy and shrink.

Misleading information comes in many forms—some more benign than others—leading to a general alienation from the body. I was told that if I made a wish while driving through a tunnel and held my breath until reaching the end, then my wish would come true. Not a good lesson about how to use the breath and body for manifesting what you desire. What were you taught about your body that still affects how you relate to it?

Added to this is the increasing challenge of staying connected to the body in a high-tech, stressful world that all but erases our animal nature. As we have evolved into high-tech beings, we have abandoned the body by living virtual lives that overemphasize the mind. Computers and automobiles dominate our lives. Physical activity falls by the wayside, as we walk less and drive more. We move less and think more. We play less and surf the Web more. Indeed, our primary forms of entertainment find us sitting in front of some kind of screen and, unfortunately, "high definition" does not refer to the effect on our muscle tone.

The influence of television on body image alone is impossible to measure, never mind how it influences the ways we talk and relate to one another. For example, I remember a particular episode of the "Ed Sullivan Show" as if it were yesterday. It was Elvis Presley's national TV debut, and the network decided to censor his shaking pelvis. What a message we baby boomers got about our lower regions that night!

Children have become experts in the virtual world, spending hours watching the tube, playing video games, e-mailing, text-messaging, and socializing on Internet sites. They hardly move as they stare at the screen. The cost of this can be seen in a group of ten-year-olds who went with my friend to the beach not long ago. The boys elected to sit in a minivan and pass on the sand and waves because they preferred playing their handheld computer Game Boys!

Evolution has taken us away from our bodies, rather than bringing us closer to them. Mihaly Csikszentmihalyi offers this perspective in his book *The Evolving Self*: "After a huge jump in evolution, organisms learned to find out what was going on at a distance from them, without having to actually feel the environment. . . . The next big advance occurred when organisms developed memory. . . . Up to this point, the processing of information was entirely *intrasomatic*, that is it took place within the body of the organism. But when speech appeared (and even more powerfully with the invention of writing), information processing became *extrasomatic*." Csikszentmihalyi adds that we now store information outside of our bodies and minds, on paper and in computers, causing us to expand our awareness but further distance ourselves from home base: our bodies.

In the seventies, many people followed in the footsteps of the Beatles and author Richard Alpert (Ram Dass) by embracing Eastern teachings. Along with the many benefits came a basic message that some people took too far: "You are not your body." Early in the movement, this admonition was misconstrued, and out-of-body experiences became a goal and measure of spiritual evolution. People's enthusiasm to advance spiritually found them dissociating from the body as if it were a mere obstacle to be overcome. What they missed altogether was the "brilliant body" as a key ally. The phrase "You are not your body" became a justification for dissociating from uncomfortable feelings.

The deeper meaning of "I am not the body" is revealed when a person begins to grasp the distinction between dissociation (denial) and transcendence. When we transcend, we discover through direct experience that we are *more* than our bodies—that we possess an indwelling divine spirit with a life beyond our flesh and mortal existence.

We are *more* than a body, of course: we are energy, consciousness, and spirit, as well as flesh and blood. When we deny the body, however, we lose touch with a key access point to that transcendent part of us. That place where our spirituality meets our humanity, where spirit resides, and where infinite energy flows is the doorway through which the miraculous can enter.

My friend Hidayat Inayat Khan, brother of the beloved and respected teacher Pir Vilayat Khan and a wise Sufi master and leader in his own right, once told me, "As much as I love Sufi teachings, I never understood when my teachers said, *you are not your body.* Here I am in one of the most beautiful settings in the world [we were at a conference in Maui and enjoying dinner along the ocean, at the Grand Wailea Hotel], and still my knee hurts as I walk. I am *so* my body, as I am not separate from what I am feeling in my knee."

The Wedge of Trauma

Traumatic events in childhood that remain unresolved also reinforce the "disconnect" between mind and body. Trauma takes many forms; physical or emotional abuse, accident or injury, natural disaster, and seeing another abused or in pain are just a few examples. For a child, such events can be difficult to cope with if an adult or older child with sufficient empathy is not available to mitigate the circumstance. If unresolved, the event lives on in our body as something incomplete. Unresolved trauma from the past then appears in the present as the body attempts to reach resolution. Once such a pattern is set up, any similarly stressful event can trigger the old pain. If the pattern involves dissociation or addictive behaviors, we either check out or reach for some substance to soothe our ragged edges. This sets the wedge of trauma firmly in place.

As pioneering endocrinologist Hans Selye explains: "Organisms show a common biological response to a wide range of unpleasant sensory or psychological experience. These are called 'stressors.' Stressors are whatever you are trying to avoid. Stressors may serve as a trigger, activating a reservoir of feelings we have avoided for years."

Separation from the body started when something happened (a stressor) that felt unfamiliar or uncomfortable, and you were not able to fully explore or express it. In the case of more serious trauma, a child may go into mild or severe shock. If the child does not receive the care and attention needed to emotionally digest what has happened, the seed of dissociation is planted.

The Distortion of Shame

On the milder end of the spectrum, the gap between body and mind stems from programming that encourages us to be quiet and repress our feelings in the interest of a stoic—or, in the child's case, well-behaved—exterior. The struggle between the free spirit to express and a conventional mind-set to repress is powerfully captured in a song you may recall by Cat Stevens titled "Father and Son," from his classic album *Tea for the Til-*

lerman. Stevens, singing both his father's and his own words, back and forth in a dialogue, explains that the moment he could talk, he was ordered to listen rather than express his desires. That conversation between them has stuck in my brain ever since. The old maxim that "children should be seen and not heard" is a bizarre idea given our natural curiosity and the expansive awareness we possess when we are young. We get the message that it isn't OK to express the feelings that arise in our bodies, and while "out of sight out of mind" may work for a time, we do pay a price. Whether emotions are avoided and discouraged for the sake of expedience or because we have yet to develop emotional literacy is a quandary beyond the scope of this book. What is important to this discussion is recognizing that we retard our natural development when we inhibit our feelings. When we invalidate vital information contained in bodily signals, we can end up with distorted perceptions.

Another factor that increases the gap between mind and body, at least in America, is the long-standing puritanical view of the body that is primarily negative. Charles Tart, psychology professor at University of California, Davis, and author of many books on human development, consciousness, and spirituality, writes, "body/instinctive development is not simply ignored in our culture, it is often badly distorted." According to Tart, the feelings of shame fostered in children when parents reject natural body functions, as well as attitudes that view bodily functions as dirty and sinful, "lead to a general neglect and rejection of the body/instinctive function that can persist into adulthood."

Spin Traps

The reason why worry kills more people than work
is that more people worry than work.

—ROBERT FROST

Most of us deal with a tremendous amount of stress due to lifestyle demands. We work long hours and schedule our rest and recreation time to the hilt. It becomes easy to ignore our bodies. We grab fast food, drive while we chow down, and chat it up on the cell phone between gulps. We sacrifice our connection with the body and its all-knowing voice by running over its vital signals with bad habits. Dr. Pamela Peeke of the University of Maryland says, "The human body was never meant to deal with prolonged chronic stress. We weren't meant to drag around bad memories, anxieties, and frustrations." Well, that's exactly what we have forced our bodies to do. Because we view stress as something to escape, we shuttle through unpleasant tasks and ignore our feelings. Conditioned thoughts and beliefs—as well as the repressed feelings and emotions that they cover up—become ingrained patterns. These patterns repeat in chronic loops that we may be largely unaware of. Even those who are aware still find it difficult to disconnect from spin thinking. As a result, we are often caught up in a spin trap with nowhere to go. These loops contribute to limiting, self-defeating, and even self-destructive behaviors that undermine our well-being and keep us from achieving our goals. Like most ingrained emotional, psychological, and behavioral patterns, spin traps repeat and produce "the same old, same old" until they are recognized, healed, and changed.

Dr. Joe Dispenza sheds interesting new light on these inner dynamics and chronic loops of thinking, feeling, and behaving in his book *Evolve Your Brain*:

> Thinking creates feeling, and then feeling creates thinking, in a continuous cycle. This loop eventually creates a particular state in the body that determines the general nature of how we feel and behave. When the body responds to a thought by having a feeling, this initiates

a response in the brain. The brain, which constantly monitors and evaluates the status of the body, notices that the body is feeling a certain way. In response to that bodily feeling, the brain generates thoughts that produce corresponding chemical messengers; you begin to think the way you are feeling.

By disconnecting from our brilliant bodies and abandoning ourselves, we lose our natural confidence. We grow more reluctant to take risks. We lose the ability to feel and acknowledge our deepest feelings and the courage to speak our truth. And we continue to deny and repress our feelings to protect ourselves. Pain, shame, fear, sadness, confusion, and aloneness are the result. Fear, denial, and disconnection from our body and our feelings become an unconscious, self-protective habit, a default response to life. The innermost self is abandoned. Instead of playing full-out, many of us begin to play it safe, or play not to lose.

The resolution to spindoctrination is to consciously get out of your head and choose whole-body consciousness. When you reconnect with your big-picture brilliance as a human being, you will heal this separation and gain the innate personal power to create the life you want and deserve. You have what you need right inside of you, and in fact, you have always had an exquisite, precision "astrolabe" right here in your body.

The integrative conversation between the mind and body can lead you back to whole-body consciousness, to your total self and your true nature. The next chapter will give you four body-mind integration tools to do just that. Life *is* a thrill ride after all, and you have been given a brilliant vehicle in which to take the journey.

Whole-Body Inquiry

*Nothing is as close to us as our body, but there is nothing else
that is close to us and about which we know so little.*

—GUNTHER VON HAGENS, creator of the "Body Worlds" exhibits

F AR FROM A mystery, whole-body consciousness is closer to
you than anything originating in the outside world—even
your name. This chapter will give you the tools to unearth
the great treasure every one of us is poised to receive simply
because we are alive at this evolutionary moment.

In much the same way as our ability to become multilingual
does not develop if we aren't exposed to different languages,
WBC does not grow if not sparked and encouraged. Expressed
another way, we've been marinated in what turns out to be
predominantly *rational-linear consciousness*, emphasizing the spe
cialized tendencies of the left hemisphere of the brain (causality,
linearity, logic, reason) at the expense of trans-rational forms
of knowing such as intuition and whole-body consciousness,
which could also be called *whole-being knowing*. To the degree
we emphasize rational development at the expense of WBC,
we limit our somatic intelligence.

Like so many of our human capacities, whole-body consciousness grows with use and becomes dormant or atrophies

when we don't exercise it. Even people schooled in mind-body integration and somatic awareness can overlook or forget to tap into this state when under stress. One client, a yoga teacher who holds a master's degree in psychology, found that simply having a name for this specialized state—whole-body consciousness—increased her ability to access it manifold. In the awakening process, naming something is an act of creation; the word is literally made flesh in your body and being. You become something different—more intelligent and more capable—simply by tapping into this dimension of who you are and always have been.

Four Tools to Activate the Brilliance of Your Body

It is of utmost importance to start exactly where you are and anchor each new increment of awareness in your body. To that end, we will begin by evaluating your current level of *body intelligence* (BQ) by utilizing the *BQ inquiry*, a simple assessment tool that I have developed and tested on thousands of clients in both one-to-one counseling and seminar settings. Most people find that simply answering the BQ inquiry questions acts like an alarm to wake up somatic intelligence and activate the "brilliant body."

Once you have completed your BQ inquiry, you are ready to dive a bit deeper and explore your *body biography*, *body personality*, and *body billboard*. Equipped with these four tools, you will begin to discover your current state of body-mind integration.

Awareness is what we're after here. The BQ inquiry is nothing like those IQ tests that tax your brain and require hard work and steadfast focus. This is awareness work that invites a soft focus and trains you in self-reflective processes that lead to breakthroughs and positive change.

Juan, a physician who attended one my seminars, had just such a breakthrough when his BQ was sparked, and he exponentially increased his level of body-mind integration and, in turn, his congruence.

Juan wanted to build his struggling medical practice. He held six degrees from his native South America and was incredibly skilled at diagnosing complex medical issues with keen accuracy. I asked Juan to stand in front of the group and speak about his services. From the back of the room, I watched intently and suddenly realized why this brilliant physician had only a handful of patients. Juan spoke with a scowl on his face, looking down at the floor with his arms folded. His stance belied his words, as he said, "I am devoted to the total well-being of my patients." When he finished, I asked the people sitting in the room to raise a hand if they would call Juan when in need of medical attention. Not a single hand went up.

Juan was broadcasting tension through his body, while his words were emphasizing well-being. His body language and his message were incongruent. I stood next to Juan and asked him to close his eyes and see himself working with a patient while resting in the place in his heart that had inspired him to become a doctor. I then invited him to address the group again and, on a hunch, suggested he speak in his native language.

This time, Juan made eye contact with everyone, used his arms expressively, and literally bounced up out of his formerly rigid knees. Even his stiff shoulders relaxed and fell a full inch. As he spoke slowly in Spanish, his facial expressions became animated, his voice expressed his passion, and he became genuinely excited to share his expertise. When he finished, I asked the group, "How many of you understand Spanish?" No one raised a hand. Then I asked, "How many of you would go to Juan if you had a medical need?" Everyone in the room raised their hand.

We all have this tendency to broadcast our inner—and often subconscious—reality to the world. Before we explore this idea further, let's take a step back and lay some groundwork. We'll start with the BQ inquiry to awaken your brilliant body and make an assessment of where you are now. Then you will have a chance to complete your body biography; this will help you understand how you got where you are. Then we'll look through a slightly different lens—the body personality. Last, we'll look at what I call your "body billboard" and explore the process by which it becomes congruent with your highest aspirations and goals.

How High Is Your BQ?

Rather than give you a lengthy intelligence test full of multiple choice and true-or-false-type questions that you then tally up to determine your score, I offer these questions as an invitation to discover something new about your brilliant body. You'll answer three groups of questions. The point of this exercise is not to judge or evaluate your BQ; it is to stimulate your BQ. There are no right or wrong answers, so have fun with this.

BQ Inquiry: *How Connected Are You with Your Body?*

1. How often do you notice the quality of your breathing? Right now, are you aware if your breathing is shallow or deep? Is it relaxed? Short or choppy?
2. How often do you consciously take a moment to pause and simply witness what you are doing? Do you ever pause and take a full, deep breath or two before acting on an impulse or sudden surge of anger?
3. How often do you scan your body and connect with how you are really feeling? For example, do you notice when

your belly is tight or your shoulders crunched? Are you aware of it when your jaw is clenched or when your hands tighten into a fist?

BQ Inquiry: *How Alert Are You to the Signals Coming from Your Body?*

1. When you feel an uncomfortable sensation, pain, tightness, or emotion in your body, is your tendency to tune in and listen to what your body may be telling you? Do you ignore or dismiss these signals? Do you shift positions and immediately try to rid yourself of such sensations and feelings?

2. When you make decisions, whether small or large, do you take a moment to consult with your body and notice how it feels before you decide? Or do you evaluate the facts and just use your mind to decide? Do you check in with your gut? Your heart? Do you ever just get a "feeling" about something? Do you tend to notice that feeling in the moment? After the fact? Do you ignore it or act on it? Are most of your decisions a matter of using your brain and cognitive powers?

3. On a scale of one to ten, how comfortable do you generally feel in your own skin? How aware are you of your body, its signals, posture, habits, and messages that it broadcasts?

BQ Inquiry: *Are You Aware of the Dialogue You Have Going On with Your Body?*

1. Would you say you have a body-friendly vocabulary? Do you say things like "I could just kick myself for doing that," "That guy gives me a headache," or "This job makes me sick and is a big pain in the neck"? Or do you ever say harsher things like "I hate my body"?

2. If you do speak harshly to or about your body, are you aware when you say such things, or is it mostly an unconscious habit? Do you say things of that nature often? Once in a while?

3. Are you aware of congruence or incongruence between your words and your body language? Do you notice when your mouth is saying one thing and your body is communicating something completely different? Do you actually stop to notice how you are feeling when you tell someone how you're doing? How often do you catch it when you simply respond as if by reflex? Do you even stop to notice how you are in the moment when asked? Do you answer "fine" or act cheerful when you don't feel that way inside?

Your answers to the previous questions should give you an initial sense of whether you have a high, medium, or low BQ.

Take a moment to reflect. What did you learn from this section about your relationship with your body?

Now take several deep breaths before you move on to the next section.

The Library of Your Cells: Your Body Biography

Your entire life story is held within the library of your cells. The body biography is a BQ tool that can help you get into that library and begin to understand and interpret what you feel every day in your body. Review your body biography, and you bring conscious awareness to the secrets and wisdom stored there. Even if you have erased a biographical event from your mind—intentionally or unintentionally—your body remembers what happened. Your body was there (as was pure awareness) even if your mind dissociated from what was happening. For many people, this review of personal history opens the door to profound healing and growth.

Juan found the body biography exercise quite revealing. A number of experiences he had when he first came to the United States—people talking to him very slowly as if he might not understand English, and not being selected for a prestigious hospital position—had led him to believe that his American peers viewed him as less intelligent because of his accent. He feared that his ethnic background and immigrant status would deter his professional advancement even though he was extremely bright and had graduated from medical school at the top of his class. Although Juan never sat down and consciously planned it out, he developed a strategy to handle this perceived threat. He summed up that strategy this way: "To make it in America, I need to prove how much smarter I am than everyone else." This in turn caused him to lead with his head instead of his heart while adopting a fairly rigid physical stance.

The body biography can also help you understand feelings you may have felt throughout your life in a larger context. Often, feelings seem to come out of nowhere for no particular rhyme or reason. Yet the body, like the heart, "has reasons of which reason knows nothing," to use the famous words of Blaise Pascal. The body biography can help you see the bigger picture and clue you in on the unseen reasons for what you may be feeling. Often, this little bit of added perspective makes all the difference in your ability to respond effectively in the moment.

Before each of the instructions that follow, take a slow, deep breath, inhaling through your nose and out through your mouth, releasing the breath with an audible sigh. After you read each instruction, close your eyes and observe what happens in your body. Take a moment to focus on any sensations that occur and notice if any images or body memories arise. Feel free to move and make sounds or do whatever your body wants to do as you contemplate each event. Then, open your eyes and write down what you have noticed before going on to the next instruction.

Once again, you may not have a conscious memory associated with each life event listed below. Nonetheless, tune in to your body's reactions. Use imagination where appropriate. For instance, your imagination can likely conjure a sense of how your parents felt when you were conceived. What is important to remember is that even where conscious memory (visual, auditory, kinesthetic) is scant or nonexistent, your body *is* there through every moment of your life, and it has a record of everything.

Imagine how your parents were feeling when you were conceived. _____

_____

_____

_____

Imagine how your mom felt when she found out she was pregnant with you. _____

_____

_____

_____

Imagine how your dad felt when he found out your mom was pregnant with you. _____

_____

_____

_____

Imagine the many feelings you felt while in your mom's belly. _____

_____

_____

_____

Imagine how you felt when your mother went into labor.

_____

_____

_____

_____

Imagine how you felt while being born. _____

_____

_____

_____

Imagine the first time you were fed (formula or breast milk). _____

_____

_____

_____

Imagine times in your crib, stroller, and baby swing. ____

_____

_____

_____

Imagine how you felt when you were placed in the arms of someone outside your immediate family. ____ ___

_____

_____

_____

Imagine how you felt when you took your first step. _____

_____

_____

_____

Imagine how you felt when you fell down after your first
few steps. _____

_____

_____

_____

Imagine how you felt when you were being toilet trained.

_____

_____

_____

_____

Imagine or remember a time when you heard a loud or
unexpected noise, such as a thunderstorm, sonic boom, air
raid, or fire alarm; or—if you live in earthquake country—first felt the ground shake beneath you. _____

_____

_____

_____

Imagine or remember a time when you skinned a knee,
banged your chin, burned your skin, broke a bone, or cut
yourself. _____

_____

_____

_____

Now, take a moment and let any other memories from your first years of life surface.

Now move forward in time; you're a little older—age four or five, and on up into your teens. Let's continue to explore your body biography.

Remember the First Time:

You went to a playgroup, started nursery school, or entered kindergarten _____

_____

_____

_____

You were acknowledged by a group of people (applauded for acting in a school play, cheered for hitting a home run, etc.) _____

_____

_____

_____

You felt proud of something you had done _____

_____

_____

_____

You got into a physical fight or witnessed one _____

_____

_____

_____

You went to the doctor _____

_____

_____

_____

You went to the dentist _____

_____

_____

_____

You went to your first boy-girl party _____

_____

_____

_____

You had a date to a party or dance _____

_____

_____

_____

You had sexual feelings _____

_____

_____

_____

You had sexual contact with someone _____

_____

_____

_____

(Women) You had your first menstrual flow _____

_____

_____

_____

(Men) You had your first wet dream _____

_____

_____

_____

Someone close to you died _____ _____

_____

_____

_____

Take a few moments to reflect on any other childhood memories that arise. _____ _____

_____

_____

_____

Now, moving forward in time again, think back to:

The first time you fell in love ___ _____

_____

_____

_____

Your high school prom _____

_____

_____

_____

Your first job ___ ___ ___ _____

_____

_____

_____

Opening your first bank account and/or starting to pay bills _____ _____

_____

_____

_____

Renting your first apartment or house _____

_____

_____

_____

Experiencing rejection or failure in business _____

_____

_____

_____

Having a big success in business _____

_____

_____

_____

Losing a sweetheart or being rejected in a relationship you
valued _____

_____

_____

_____

Your marriage ceremony _____

_____

_____

_____

The birth of your first child _____

_____

_____

Your high school reunion _____

_____

_____

_____

Your biggest celebration or party _____ _____

_____

_____

_____

Your most exciting vacation or traveling experience _____

_____

_____

_____

Your worst memory _____

_____

_____

_____

Your best memory _____

_____

_____

_____

Your scariest experience _____

_____

_____

_____

Your happiest experience _____

_____

_____

_____

Your silliest experience ____ _____

_____

_____

_____

Your saddest experience _____

_____

_____

_____

Your angriest moment _____

_____

_____

_____

Your most peaceful, contented experience _____

_____

_____

_____

When you were the most proud of yourself _____

_____

_____

_____

Now take a few moments to notice how you are feeling. What is happening in your body? What did you learn? You may discover that memories begin to bubble up over the coming days. Your dreams may give you more information as well.

A few years ago, I saw a Disney film that beautifully illustrates the dramatic effect biographical events can have on the course of a person's life. In *The Kid* (2000), Bruce Willis plays the part of Russ, who is about to have his fortieth birthday. Russ feels and looks like a phony at the outset of the movie; his life is stressful and empty. Hollywood magic allows Russ to pay a visit to his past, and he has the opportunity to relive specific events that led to his unhappy existence. First Russ sees himself as an eight-year-old boy getting into a fight with the school bullies. Then he watches as his dad blames him for his dying mother's illness and orders him to stop crying. Willis, as the thirty-nine-year-old Russ, watches a younger Russ hold in all of his emotions and become a workaholic who is self-conscious about a nervous twitch in his eye.

The film graphically represents a basic tenet of body-oriented therapy: when we reexperience difficult or traumatic childhood events and release repressed emotions that have been stored in the body, healing can occur. That healing, for Russ, results in the disappearance of his facial twitch. A changed man, he begins to take action. The amount of love, happiness, and peace he can experience in his life dramatically increases.

This movie illustrates the benefit that comes with knowing your body biography. Looking into your personal history facilitates full understanding of the "what" and "how" behind limiting beliefs you may be clinging to. By addressing what happened in the past that shaped his disposition and behavior, Russ realizes that he has more options than he thought.

Each Body Has a Unique Signature: Your Body Personality

Your body is always communicating and sending out signals as to your state of mind and body—whether you are aware of it or not. In any given moment, your state is expressed through your unique body personality.

Consider the following scenario: You're at a holiday gathering, chatting with friends. You have an unmet deadline at work that you have decided to simply forget about for the evening. You put your best foot forward, don your "Everything's great!" persona, and act jovial like everyone else. You're not

consciously thinking about the deadline—nonetheless, it is
wreaking havoc in your body and your feelings at a subliminal
level. Your stomach is queasy. Your eyes are blinking. You are
tapping your foot nervously under the table. Your breathing is
restless and shallow. Your chest is a bit sunken. You are tentative and shut down despite occasional outbursts of laughter and
a hearty remark here and there. And while you are somewhat
aware of the agitated state you are in, you are largely unaware
of the hundred little ways you are broadcasting it to everyone
at the party.

Versions of this scene occur all the time. You might be in a
similar state while at an important business meeting, on a first
date, celebrating an anniversary with your spouse, or playing
ball in the park with your kids. "Everywhere you go, there you
are," as they say.

An individual's "personality" is comprised of his or her
attitudes, behavioral patterns, emotional responses, interests,
social roles, and other individual traits that endure. Just as you
express yourself through a composite of the various psychological aspects of self just mentioned, you also express yourself
through a distinct *body* personality. You can readily validate
this by beginning to notice the people closest to you. Take
particular note of how you recognize someone you know in a
crowd. The part of your brain that accomplishes this complex
task knows exactly how to scan a large group of humans and
pick out a loved one based on the way he or she walks.

You can have a real field day watching body personalities at
a class reunion. Individual qualities and quirks that make each
person unique are fairly transparent when we are all stumbling
and fumbling our way through high school. When you haven't
seen someone for a decade or more, those unique mannerisms
practically jump out at you. A toss of the head or a signature
hand gesture can broadcast a person's identity from across the

room. Next time you get invited to a reunion, go and watch the body personalities on parade.

Some people have such a distinct way of being in a body that we call them "characters." Watch any brilliant character actor and you will see a highly specialized craft. Take Jack Nicholson in *One Flew Over the Cuckoo's Nest*, for example. Better yet, consider several of his acclaimed roles side by side. Nicholson's unique genius gives him total mastery over a host of minute mannerisms and eccentricities that can be shuffled and dealt anew to create quite a distinct body personality time and again.

Tina came to see me because she sensed her self-esteem issues were sabotaging both her personal life and real estate business. As we talked, I watched her body language and noticed a peculiar mannerism that she repeated over and over. At fairly regular intervals, she would bring her hands in front of her and move them from one side of her body to the other as though she were moving an object. Within a period of thirty minutes, she did this at least a dozen times. When I commented on what I noticed, she looked surprised.

I then invited Tina to breathe and become fully aware of her body, and this gesture in particular. Then I mimicked her repetitive gesture and asked her to exaggerate it deliberately several times. When she did, a light went on immediately. Just as we can be blind to personality characteristics others witness in us all the time, she had been blind to this expression of her body personality.

After several repetitions, tears began rolling down her cheeks. After several more repetitions, she shared her memories: "I was four years old when my mother gave birth to twins. I went from having all of her attention to having very little of it. She completely shifted all of her focus and love from me to them. I felt angry, sad, and confused, but I had no way to express those feelings. I felt invisible, like I'd been set aside, and on top of it, I felt guilty for having those feelings about my little brothers." I encouraged Tina to feel her mixed emotions of sadness and anger and to express them freely through her body while exaggerating her movements. Her posture changed completely as she gave herself permission to embody the sadness and bewilderment of that young girl. Sadness took over her face, and then suddenly anger erupted from the very core of her. She shouted, "I'm here too! I need your attention!" Almost immediately, a tangible wave of relief moved through her body. She opened her eyes and smiled. "Hey, that's right. I do deserve to have people's attention, and I *do* deserve to be here." I had her continue to speak those words over and over while tuning in to her body. After several moments, she said, "A part of me that gave up a long time ago feels like it just came alive!"

Tina hadn't realized that her hurt and anger from many years ago expressed itself through that gesture, and that each time she did that, she reinforced the four-year-old Tina's point of view. Her subconscious was saying through her body, "I can be displaced or set aside at any moment." With increased awareness, Tina was able to connect the dots between a previously unconscious gesture and suppressed feelings that contributed to her low self-esteem. The gesture had captured, like a snapshot, a vital piece of her that now freed her to build a sense of personal worth rather than set herself and her value aside.

Working with video is a great way to get in touch with your body personality. It can be quite a surprise to suddenly get a clear look at the way others see you. Most of us are only subliminally aware of the small or large mannerisms, facial expressions, physical gestures, and various postural cues that express through our body all the time. And yet other people see and are responding to all of those cues and expressions every day. In fact, to others, those ways of being in your body are a major part of how they identify you as you. This alone makes it hard to resist investigating! But more important, raising awareness of your body personality can reap many benefits, including these:

- Enhanced appearance
- Improved breathing, movement patterns, and skeletal health
- More productive business and social exchanges, with fewer embarrassing moments
- Increased self-love and empathy for others
- Reduced shame and guilt about body habits
- Minimized stress through using your body more creatively
- Increased self-awareness and ability to make a contribution
- Increased joy

Being *all* of who you are—rather than being whoever conditioning and habits have caused you to be unconsciously—is a great boon that comes with inhabiting your brilliant body.

Like Tina, my body personality was all but invisible to me until I made it a practice to watch others' body language. I began to realize just how powerful this dimension of who we are truly is and started to investigate my own body gestures. Once I did this, my own body personality began to reveal itself. Like a detective, I became alert to many small clues I hadn't noticed before. Awareness moved into my vocal cords; I began to hear a certain tension in my voice that carried a specific meaning—an attitude or disposition that communicated as clearly as my words. For example, if I felt nervous or excited during a discussion, I would begin to talk very quickly and sometimes interrupt another person in midsentence. Upon investigating this, I saw that it clearly carried a message: *I have something urgent to say, and you need to hear it now!* A whole postural dynamic accompanied this tendency, too. I would lean forward as my eyes made a jutting motion. My body personality turned out to be a bit pushy! Other unconscious habits came to my attention as I continued to investigate my body personality. For example, I would clench my jaw and smile when covering up anger, and my eyes would wander back and forth when I was unsure of myself in conversation.

Now it's your turn. The best place to begin your investigation into your body personality is in your face. Pay attention to how you use your facial muscles. Be alert and aware of how a particular smile or glance is linked to an outcome. Facial expressions often serve a subconscious agenda. A smile can be used to accomplish many things. Spend a day or two simply observing what you do with your face. Then expand your investigation to the whole of your body. Notice how your mood affects your gait at different times. Notice how what you are thinking in any given moment affects your posture. Investigate also how you use your gaze. Pay close attention to what you are saying to another by shifting your gaze or looking off into space. Likewise, the way you position your body or tilt your head shows the world what you think about yourself in relation to others. All these little nuances make up your distinct body personality. More often than not, if they remain unconscious, these habitual ways of being act as a cover for your authentic self.

Pay close attention to repetitive body gestures as well. Better yet, ask someone close to you to impersonate you. Specifically ask that person to mimic your gestures and attempt to duplicate your carriage. This type of feedback gives you valuable information and helps you learn more about yourself. From a platform of increased awareness, you can begin to identify aspects of your personality that are ingrained and habituated yet out of sync with the person you are today.

For example, let's say you discover that you tend to hunch over when speaking to people. You tune in to the emotional state that accompanies that posture and note that it has a sad and insecure feel to it. You are familiar with this facet of yourself and can trace it back to grammar school when you felt inept at math. Armed with this awareness, you now have a choice whether to alter this aspect of your body personality—or not. You are no longer on automatic pilot, sending out the message *I'm sad and insecure.*

Get in touch with your body personality by becoming what I playfully call a "BP detective" for a while. We have lots of fun with this one in seminars, tracking down what we do unconsciously with our bodies and learning what it means. The practice always leads to a satisfying sense of mind-body connectedness.

You have many "warning lights" and "gauges" in your body-mind that tell you what you need to know to live authentically and effectively. Like learning to read the dashboard in your car, you can learn to pay attention to your inner gauges. Most of us have a felt sense in the gut that lets us know—with a nonverbal inner "yes" or "no!"—what is most real and true. We may have learned to override that knowing. Now is the time to reclaim it. The more you read these signs and heed your inner nudges, the more they will provide that just-right guidance that highlights old ways of being that are now ripe for change.

By now your body awareness and your BQ have begun to expand. You understand that your body has a history that is expressed through a distinct personality. You are beginning to sense that this body of yours is much more than a vehicle to push toward your goals. And yet your body *is* the vehicle through which you accomplish or fall short of those goals. So let's see how these first three tools—BQ, body history, and body personality—work together like easel, paint, and paper to make up your body billboard.

Your Most Decisive Communication: Your Body Billboard

We all walk around wearing our own "billboard." This is our overall expression—the countless messages we continually communicate with our body. For most of us, this is largely unconscious whole-body communication. It includes vocal tones and inflections, physical gestures, postures, involuntary movements, breathing, pacing of speech, and numerous other subtle and not-so-subtle signals that make up your body personality. Your body billboard is essentially the summary statement of the three areas you have just explored. It communicates in a flash exactly how you feel about yourself in all situations. It carries shades of unprocessed feelings and wounds, traumas you may not have resolved, and other forms of baggage you might be carrying around. It is your overall expression, your subliminal curriculum vitae, your self-advertisement to the world.

Your body billboard is not static, of course, and it is important to note that we are speaking metaphorically here when we call this facade a billboard. The beauty of metaphor lies in its ability to help you see what you otherwise cannot—in this case, the incongruence between actions and words. We generally tend to be unaware of this incongruence, due to the pervasive body-mind disconnection. As a result, our total communication to others is often skewed and confusing. Your billboard is probably your most decisive communication. Visual, nonverbal, and largely subliminal, it is an essential communication most hidden to your self and most visible to others. *Your billboard always expresses who you are being in the moment.* Its messages may completely contradict what you communicate with your social persona and say with your words.

You can't stop your billboard from broadcasting, even for an instant. When what you are feeling, thinking, *and* speaking are incongruent, your billboard could be broadcasting "spin"—mixed messages that confuse, mislead, or simply ring untrue and are therefore off-putting to others. You may not be aware that you are doing this, for the most part. If you broadcast mixed messages, you'll get mixed messages in return. That incongruence generally results in confusion, difficulty, and self-sabotage. The messages we broadcast on our billboard can mean the difference between success and failure, intimacy and isolation, gaining recognition and being overlooked.

Saying one thing and sending the opposite message through your billboard is classic "spin talk." No matter how sincere your intentions may be, this approach is ultimately ineffective because it denies your authentic self and needs.

Conversely, when we are consciously in our bodies, aware of what we're feeling and communicating, we begin to function with natural confidence, power, and efficiency and connect more authentically with others.

Juan had a huge breakthrough when he realized why his billboard was so different from his words. His early experiences in the United States, when he feared being judged less intelligent by his American peers, had colored his billboard. The resulting belief—*I have to prove I'm smarter than everyone else*—was the primary message he broadcast, and this was sabotaging his practice. Once this unconscious stance became conscious and the emotional gestalt was cleared, his new billboard

proclaimed his true intent: "I want and deserve to be successful, and I am smart enough to do it here in America." Today, Juan has two successful offices, publishes a regular newsletter, is a highly effective public speaker, and is living his dream with passion and purpose.

Begin to communicate with your whole body along more authentic lines, and your billboard will dynamically serve, rather than sabotage, your best intentions and goals.

CHAPTER

≋ 4 ≋

Ready—SET—Go!

*Technique turns us from suffering and darkness to glorify
every aspect of life through contact with our inner wisdom.*

—THE *Yoga Sutras*

*Self-reliance is the only road to true freedom, and
being one's own person is its ultimate reward.*

—A. PATRICIA SAMPSON, director of World Alive Ministries

A LITTLE BOY STANDS holding his father's hand while waiting in line at the carnival. He shuffles his feet with eager
anticipation of his favorite summertime treat—a snow cone.
The father smiles as he remembers his own boyhood and the
irresistible draw of the sugary-sweet, brightly colored ice. A
moment later, the boy pulls his hand away and starts to scratch
his head.

Father asks, "I notice you keep scratching your head today,
son. Why?"

"Because I'm the only one who knows it itches," says the
boy.

The little boy's answer is profound, because it illustrates an
obvious fact that we tend to lose touch with by the time we are
adults. As the only resident inside your body, only you have access
to the vast library of emotions and sensations inside your flesh.
Getting in touch with the physical dimension of your being is

the single most powerful way to enter the immediate moment. Enter the moment *as it is*, and you increase your capacity for making clear choices tenfold and maybe even hundredfold.

Access the Now with SET (Self-Evident Truth)

You can experience the power of fully entering the moment with a simple body-awareness exercise that I have developed. The technique is called "SET" (for self-evident truth), and it allows you to land smack in the here and now by focusing your full attention on your physical and emotional body.

Here's an example: Suppose it's a day when you are slightly sad and tense, and someone asks, "How are you?" Nine times out of ten, you will probably answer, "Fine." If you were aware of your actual experience, you might say, "I feel sad, and my chest is tight." Depending on who asked the question, you may or may not want to explain why you are sad. Either way, how you are feeling in the moment is sad and tight. No one can argue with that subjective truth, because no one else lives in your body. Like the little boy who reached up to scratch his head, you are the only one who knows what you feel; yet, you are most likely out of touch with that, as discussed in Chapter 2. The SET technique reinstates your sovereignty by reinforcing and proving to you again and again that you do in fact know exactly what you feel in your body.

SET gets you out of your head and puts you into direct contact with your whole body, increasing awareness and building BQ each time you do it. This simple six-step exercise can be used for relaxation, physical and emotional healing, and intuitive decision making. With practice, you will begin to sense subtle shades of feeling and sensation in your body that you may not have been aware of before. The more you "talk" to your body and listen to its self-evident truths, the more these visceral nuances will reveal your body's unique vocabulary.

You learned your ABCs in school in order to read; now you are going to learn a somatic, or bodily, alphabet made up of sensations and feelings instead of letters. Physiologically, this highly personal alphabet consists of pathways in your nervous system that you can discover and become familiar with over time. All it takes is practice, and—as you will soon discover— the immediate results are peace of mind and clarity. This is self-empowerment at a physical level.

Ready to learn how to initiate SET? The six-step exercise that follows draws from both Eastern spiritual traditions and Western psychology. While SET may seem simple, the effects in terms of body-mind integration can be quite profound. Here we go:

1. Commit. Commit to place all of your attention on yourself for the next two minutes. Point or imagine pointing at your chest and say this out loud or silently: "I am willing and ready to focus my attention on my body and feel what it is feeling right now."

2. Breathe. Take three slow, deep, full breaths in through your nose and out through your mouth. Relax and fill your belly on each inhalation, then release the breath slowly and let your jaw drop open as you exhale. Keep the out-breath natural, like a soft sigh. Release the breath out through your throat, careful not to force it through your lips by blowing or pushing your exhale out. Breathe in and out rhythmically, and let whatever wants to happen in your body happen. If your head wants to lean forward, let it. If your hand tightens, let it.

3. Scan. Notice what is happening in your body. Are you gripping this book tightly, or are your hands relaxed? Are you squinting or straining in any way? Are you tensing up while you read? Are your shoulders and neck and jaw relaxed? Do you feel any emotion? Notice, don't analyze. Close your eyes and scan your body. Reopen your eyes when you are ready.

4. Declare. State aloud what you notice; declare the truth of your body. For instance, you might say, "I am noticing that my breath is shallow and my fingers are tingly." Or, "I am noticing how relaxed my belly and chest feel." Go ahead and say whatever comes up when you look within: "I am noticing _____."

5. Witness. Sometimes when you declare your self-evident truth, body sensations begin to change. If this happens, simply observe and witness the change. If you said, "I notice that my jaw is tight," this acknowledgement may actually stimulate relaxation or increased energy flow in the jaw. Or another sensation may suddenly arise in a completely different part of your body. For instance, your fist may be tight, and when you declare this, a rush of anger could erupt and cause you to grit your teeth.

6. Act. Now, take an action that benefits you right now. For instance, if your self-evident truth is that you aren't breathing deeply, take some deep breaths. If you notice that your shoulders are raised, relax them and let them drop.

How are you now? Whatever you experienced, you just had a conscious, *whole-body* experience. You raised your body awareness. What was the quality of your breathing, and how did it change as the exercise progressed? What physical sensations did you experience? Did you get hot or cold? Did you feel tingling, numbness, or involuntary movements, such as twitching? Did you become aware of inner dialogue or hear someone else's words? Did any memories or images surface? Did you see, smell, or taste anything while your eyes were closed?

SET is the ideal "pregame warm-up" for any activity. You can do it before an appearance, a meeting, or a social event to become instantly more present and self-aware. SET is completely user-friendly; you don't need special machines or environments.

Once you learn the simple steps, you can do this practice any-where, anytime. The more often you actually do the exercise rather than just read about it, the more your body intelligence will increase. Reading about working out doesn't build muscle mass—going to the gym and lifting weights does.

Let's look at an example. Suppose you're the regional sales manager at a large firm and your monthly sales figures are due by the end of the day. Someone asks, "How are you?" Without the benefit of a practice like SET, you might answer, "I will be fine once Sara gets that big order signed and on my desk."

Notice the difference? Rather than share a self-evident truth—the subjective what's-so that is real and true in the moment—this type of response takes you out of the moment, and out of your body, into the future. A mental picture of what you desire in the future acts like an overlay on top of how you actually feel. This re-creates and reinforces the fissure between mind and body. We override BQ whenever we ignore or over-look the mind–body chasm this way. What you miss when you deny the body and short-circuit its brilliance is the refined awareness that comes with a body and mind working together to grasp a much bigger picture than either alone can see.

Choosing to practice SET is a choice to reunite your body and mind and refine your awareness by accessing and increas-ing BQ. In much the same way that an archery buff increases his hand-eye coordination every time he pulls the arrow back in the bow, you increase your body-mind coordination and grow BQ every time you get in touch with your inner world using SET. The archer uses his outer senses: his eyes zero in on the target; his sense of touch knows just how to hold the arrow; and his ears listen to the stretch of the bow and the whoosh of the arrow as it flies. Sight, taste, smell, touch, and hearing are called *exteroceptive* senses—these tell us all about the outer world. But most people don't know that we also have *interoceptive* senses, which allow you to register what is happening inside the body. Practice SET, and you engage these inner senses and increase BQ, just as the archer increases his skill each time he steps up and takes aim at a target.

> *The body is anchored in the here and now while*
> *the mind travels into the past and future.*
>
> —BUDDHA

Let's follow Buddha's line of thought and develop the anchor metaphor for a moment. Where does a sailor drop anchor? In a safe harbor—when and where he finds a secure bay away from the winds and the swells and the depths of the open sea. And what does he do while anchored? He engages his navigation skills: he reviews his charts, checks his course and his compass, and makes clear choices based on what he learns. This is not to say that he doesn't check his compass or his charts while under sail; he just does it with less to distract him when he is safely anchored in a place of respite. The demands of the open sea are not consuming his attention when he is inside the bay; he is calm and able to consider his options carefully. This relaxed perspective is what you stand to gain with SET. See if you can sense the difference in the examples below.

Question (addressed to regional director by member of his sales team): *How are you?*

1. Last month our sales were lousy. Jack was way under quota in June, and our whole district was down 20 percent.
2. I'll be fine when Erica closes that deal and hands over a purchase order for fifty units.
3. I'm feeling excited about a presentation I'm making today. I also notice a bit of pressure in my head.

Notice that in examples 1 and 2 above, his mind projected itself out of the present and into the past or future. The answer is less immediate, and the sales manager lacks presence. From within a mental construct that is past- or future-oriented, he missed the moment.

One of my heroes is Stevie Wonder. I have been a fan since I saw him with the Motown Revue in 1962. Besides being a front-row ticket holder at several of his concerts and an avid listener, I also have been deeply influenced by many of his lyrics. For instance, his song "Pastime Paradise," where he asserts that we spend most of our lives in our past and future paradises, helped me see how I was doing both. I realized this tendency to abandon what we feel in the moment in favor of glorifying our past or idyllic futures can cause so many of us to avoid what is happening right now. Happiness, pleasure, and joy cannot be found in the past or the future, and the same is true for success and achievement. Past and future are mental constructs; experience only ever happens in the present. This doesn't mean we can't plan for the future or reflect on the past, but planning and reflecting always happen in the here and now.

Living in the Beam

SET allows you to stop spin thoughts immediately and enter the now. When you're truly in the now, there is no stress and no threat you cannot handle. No need to add something extra—you are just you in your natural state, certain of what you are certain of and curious about what you have yet to discover. Think about it: When a real threat occurs, you rise to the occasion and handle it, more often than not. Whether it's a fire, flood, or SUV swerving into your lane on the freeway, your body is well equipped with the right reflexes and resources to handle the threat. It's the threats that live only in your mind that cost you peace of mind and joy. Fall into spin, and you lose perspective—productivity and presence are sacrificed. Bringing yourself back into the moment using SET is a deliberate choice to stand beneath the bright beam of awareness that is whole-body consciousness.

How You Can Use SET to Stop the Spin

...... ≩ Silicon Valley, California, March 2006 ≩ ......

Carl is sitting on the outdoor lawn of his software company's luxurious campus, enjoying the first breath of spring, when the grapevine delivers the shocking news: *we've been acquired!* A new engineer fresh out of college, Carl is stunned. He's been with the company less than three months; he is almost sure to get canned. The messenger continues: "The CEO's office just announced that we will be closing temporarily, then reopening and downsizing." Carl's imagination immediately starts constructing the worst-case scenario: *If I get laid off, I'm dead in the water. . . . I'll never find a position this prestigious. I haven't even been here long enough to collect unemployment. . . .* Caught in the cyclone of a spin trap, Carl slumps and watches his career and his future sink like the *Titanic*. He stands up and walks around the park like a man who is completely lost. He wanders toward the coffee kiosk and orders a double cappuccino by rote—"make it wet, please." He stares blankly at the barista while she steams the milk, and mindlessly reaches for his Blackberry. He gives it a voice command: *call Sisgold.*

Carl was at a choice point. Fortunately, he was sufficiently aware of that fact to reach for his cell phone and ask for support. I listened to his report and asked him, "What's your body telling you?" Then I reminded him, "This is an opportunity to practice SET and stop your spin thoughts in their tracks." That simple wake-up call was all he needed to disengage from a catastrophic thinking pattern. Rather than stress over what he could not control (the economy, the restructuring of his company, an uncertain future), Carl chose to focus on what he could control—where he placed his attention, which of his thoughts he took seriously, and what course of action he would choose to follow.

Carl had practiced SET in the past, and he knew how to access whole-body consciousness. Like a pre-set on the car radio, he could readily tune in to WBC and tune out the swirling spin thoughts. He took a few deep breaths and embraced what he was feeling: fear in his chest and belly, tension in his jaw, anger, confusion, and sadness. Accessing the self-evident truth of the moment helped him realize that the tales he was spinning in his mind—*I'm going to lose my first job! My career is in jeopardy*—were unproven scenarios based in fear. When he inquired deeper into his body and looked for what was fueling his fear, he found familiar feelings of helplessness. As he expressed aloud, "I feel helpless," waves of energy and a swirl of sensations coursed through his body. He took action and shook his body until he felt relaxed. In that state of relaxed clarity, he realized that he really wasn't helpless at all. With the shift to WBC, Carl regained perspective and felt his confidence return. His outlook refreshed, he was able to step up to the choice point with a clear advantage. He was *in the beam*.

≡ Software Engineering Department, the Same Day ≡

Carl walks back to his small office and savors the rest of his cappuccino as a whole new range of feelings and possibilities emerge. He considers his options and decides to be proactive rather than focus on what might or might not happen down the road. Having sorted out objective facts from fearful fictions, he sees the very real possibility that his firm could ask him to stay on. He gets in touch with a desire to take action rather than sit and wait for their decision. He goes online to one of the popular tech-head recruiting sites and begins to explore other career opportunities right away. He discovers that a very prestigious software engineering firm that has its corporate office nearby is looking for a designer with his qualifications. In his mind's eye, he sees himself walking down the street on his lunch hour to pop in on the human resources department. He reads that they require appointments, but when he checks in with his body, he gets a green light and decides to visit unannounced.

When he walks into the firm, the receptionist informs him that it will be impossible to talk to someone without an appointment. Undeterred and unstoppable, he takes the elevator up to the recruiting suite and speaks to a young man at the front desk, explaining that he knows it's a bit unorthodox to approach them this way but believes he would be a great asset to their firm. He hands over his résumé and asks for an interview. One of the firm's senior managers happens to be nearby and overhears the conversation. He appreciates Carl's directness and invites him into a private side office for an on-the-spot interview. They have a brief, lively conversation, and Carl is invited to return for a formal interview the following week.

In a matter of hours, Carl turned what he had initially perceived as a disaster into an exhilarating adventure. In the long run, the disaster turned out to be a gift. Carl not only found himself in a new and more prestigious position, he also found himself the recipient of a substantial raise, a bonus plan, and a free parking spot, to boot.

The power of choice that was presented to Carl is available to all of us, even in moments that seem the darkest and most challenging. We all have what it takes to change our consciousness and behaviors at will. It starts with allowing our bodies to temper the wind and waves that constantly batter us around in the sea of the mind.

Your Body as a Thought Monitor

*He who cannot change the very fabric of his thought will never be
able to change reality, and will never, therefore, make any progress.*

—ANWAR SADAT, *In Search of Identity*

My work with people over the years has shown me the truth of
Sadat's statement. When you become aware of the cause-and-
effect relationship between your thoughts and your experience, you can become the director of your own movie rather
than a character in somebody else's unfolding drama. This is
what is meant by self-reliance.

Let's look at self-reliance from another perspective. America's founding fathers spoke of truths that were self-evident at a
societal level, and in so doing, formed a democratic system that
gave people the power to actively participate in governance. In
this way, they championed self-reliance. On a personal level,
being self-reliant doesn't mean being a solitary warrior or a
lone ranger who adopts a "me against the world" attitude. I
turn to coaches, consultants, and even a Hawaiian *kahuna* from
time to time. Likewise, I enjoy taking weekend workshops and
seminars on occasion. Ultimately, however, I do not depend
on outside counsel to guide my decisions, nor do I depend
on workshops to keep me inspired and on track. I rely on my
innate intelligence and the brilliance of my body to guide my
choices and to help me monitor my thoughts.

Over the years I've heard many clients complain of the
seemingly inevitable downturn that comes after they've
attended a motivational seminar. Maybe you've had this experience as well: You attend a weekend workshop that gets you
all pumped up, you ride high for a few days or weeks, and then
you realize you haven't changed a bit. It's the same old, same
old. So you buy a set of CDs, you take a monthly refresher

course, or join the seminar leader's volunteer staff in an effort to maintain your new edge. What has yet to emerge is complete self-reliance. Our whole discussion of self-evident truth in the first half of this chapter, including the practice of coming into the moment at a bodily level using the SET technique, is the foundation upon which to build self-reliance.

The next step in building up from that foundation is to steadily progress toward your goals. This requires dedication and a specific practice. Follow-through is key, as is consistency. Jonathan Haidt, one of the founders of the positive psychology movement, speaks to this at length in his seminal book, *The Happiness Hypothesis*. Throughout the book, Haidt uses the analogy of an elephant and rider to illustrate how the mind is divided in such a way that it often is in conflict. This quality of being divided is why it's so difficult to make positive changes stick. Haidt writes:

> Yet, if you have ever achieved such dramatic insights into your own life and resolved to change your ways or your outlook, you probably found that, three months later, you were right back where you started. Epiphanies can be life-altering, but most fade within days or weeks. The rider can't just decide to change and then order the elephant to go along with the program. Lasting change can come only by retraining the elephant, and that's hard to do.

Making progress largely depends on your ability to retrain yourself. To be awake and interactive in the creative process of your life, moment by moment, thought by thought, and move by move, requires a practice or technique that you apply consistently. If you've ever trained a dog, you're not far from understanding the elephant analogy. One stern command will not do. Repeated stern commands and consistency is what teaches the dog to obey you. Likewise, your "elephant"—the reactive, spin-thinking, undisciplined mind—needs consistent retraining before you develop this quality of self-reliance.

Dr. Majid Ali, in his book *RDA: Rats, Drugs and Assumptions*, reinforces our need to be self-reliant when he states, "The goal of all disease reversal and recovery programs is to teach the patient ways of self-reliance." He also points out, "Regrettably, counseling, analysis, regression, hypnosis and bio-feedback—as they are often practiced today—sink the patient deeper and deeper into dependence on the therapist." Dr. Ali's point is well taken. It has always been my goal as a body-centered therapist to help clients develop self-reliance so their need for my coaching expires as quickly as possible. Said another way, I see my role *not* as one who fixes or heals a client; but rather as one who imparts competencies that allow the client to heal him or herself as needed, thus becoming self-reliant.

Catching the Beat

With SET you have essentially learned how to enter the moment—to "keep your eye on the ball," so to speak. The technique I am about to introduce you to will help you improve your swing, so to speak. I call this one *attituning*.

While most of us are not able to control what thoughts arise in the mind, we can learn to monitor them and choose to think in ways that move us in a positive direction. This can save a tremendous amount of wasted time and energy. The key is to pay attention to the *direction* and *progression* of your thoughts. In order to understand and grasp these two concepts—direction and progression—let's define three basic categories of thought: *upward*, *downward*, and *wayward*. These very distinctions are what helped Nancy Todd Tyner lock in on that winning edge at the poker table, and they can do the same for you.

Physicists tell us that everything in the universe continually expands and contracts. The movement in your interior world—your thoughts, feelings, and perceptions—mirrors this motion. The ancient science of self-realization known as yoga captures this same concept in the notion of ascending and descending currents.

Your body is familiar with a certain flow or influx of upward energy, and we all have a happiness "ceiling," or threshold. It may sound strange at first, but your nervous system is acclimated to a specific range of pleasure. This is similar to the homeostatic mechanism in the body that keeps you at a familiar weight, or what doctors and physiologists now call your "set point." Your emotional life is similarly maintained by a happiness set point that keeps you in a familiar range. When we hit our upward threshold, we automatically start to sink into downward energy. You've likely heard people who have extreme swings of mood refer to their inner life as an "emotional roller-coaster." You may even identify with that feeling.

Attituning can help you become conscious of the underlying process and rein in your emotions before you go too far and sabotage your progress. Here is an example of how upward, downward, and wayward thoughts play in the mind: A sales executive is driving to a customer's location to make an important presentation. She's excited, thinking that today is the day she will make that big sale. This is an upward thought. As she exits the freeway, her thoughts change direction: *But I didn't get my PowerPoint presentation updated, and the one I have isn't very strong.* This is a downward thought. Her energy shifts in a downward direction as she starts to sink into the driver's seat. She does not notice this, however, and her thoughts are on automatic pilot. She thinks, *I'm not ready. Perhaps I should call and cancel or tell them I'm sick.* This is a wayward thought.

Can you see the progression? This sort of thinking goes on all the time; it can feel like being bounced around inside a pinball machine. No wonder we want to escape. By learning to detect downward thoughts, we can begin to recognize any moment of self-sabotage and minimize its effects on the decisions we make.

Let's look at each category of thought a little closer.

Upward, Downward, and Wayward Thoughts

Upward thought is any positive thought, desire, or belief that causes an uplifting spiral of energy in your whole body, creating joy, exhilaration, and an expansion of your consciousness. Your chest expands, your heart lifts, and you carry your head higher. Upward thoughts move in the direction of greater awareness; they express your unique gifts, your higher self, and your heart's desires. A simple example of an upward thought might be this: *I want to skydive.*

Downward thought is any negative, limiting thought, desire, or belief that causes a descending, inverted spiral of energy in your body, creating stressful feelings and a contraction of your consciousness. Your chest sinks in, and the area around your heart tends to collapse. Your posture slumps, as your head, shoulders, and back form a crescent. Downward thoughts move consciousness away from awareness of your unique gifts, your higher self, and your heart's desires. Downward thoughts commonly follow upward thoughts, as an unconscious reaction to them. For example, *But I'm afraid to dive because I might get hurt.*

Wayward thought is any thought that directs attention away from the stressful situation and allows you to escape it even momentarily. The wayward thought is the mind's attempt to deal with the tension between expansion and contraction. Now your body language is confused and disjointed. Your right shoulder may dip, you may become clumsy, your eyes may dart around in their sockets, or you may even get butterflies in your tummy. If you have any active addictions to cigarettes, alcohol, food, or even shopping, you may very well begin to think about or reach for your favorite distraction. Per our example: *I don't need to skydive right now. I'll go hiking instead.*

Positive thoughts tend to generate more positive thoughts and progress in an upward direction—for a while. As mentioned above, each of us has a sort of inner barometer that keeps us from exceeding our feel-good threshold. When we hit our limit for pleasure, expansion, happiness, joy, or just plain good, good feelings, a bounce-back effect occurs, and we start to contract.

Let's return to the earlier example of the sales executive. Say she picks up her cell phone and bows out of the scheduled presentation. The pressure she was feeling is instantly relieved. That is the immediate payoff, but there is a cost involved. The opportunity to make the presentation and walk through her fear passed her by, as did a chance to do the inner work and grow from it. By learning to detect downward thoughts, we can begin to recognize any moment of self-sabotage and avoid acting on wayward thoughts that steer us away from our goals instead of toward them.

Attituning allows you to monitor and adjust your thoughts and attitudes to achieve neutral buoyancy in the flowing medium of life. The Dalai Lama said, "Negative actions invariably arise in the context of negative thoughts and emotions. Conversely, positive actions arise in the context of positive, or wholesome, thoughts and emotions." In meditation practice, you learn to establish, recognize, and trust the *witness*— that aspect of consciousness that observes thoughts as passersby without reacting to them. Attituning also develops the witness; it is an active meditation. You can use it to hit the ground running rather than allowing downward thoughts to stop you in your tracks. You simply feel your feelings and note which are upward, downward, and wayward thoughts. Witness the way in which thoughts arise and then pass away.

Here are a few more examples to further clarify these three distinct categories of thought. Take note of any recurring thought patterns of your own that these examples bring to mind.

Upward thought: I love singing and would like to take a class.

Downward thought: I have a terrible voice; I'd embarrass myself.

Wayward thought: I'll take a computer class instead.

Result: You miss an opportunity to do something you love, and reinforce a limiting belief.

Upward thought: I'd like to go to that party and meet someone new.

Downward thought: I feel so awkward in social situations.

Wayward thought: I'll just stay home and watch TV.

Result: You miss an opportunity to socialize —and possibly even meet someone great—while reinforcing the belief that you don't like parties.

Every moment presents a choice to expand or contract. When you access whole-body consciousness, you can begin to feel this in your body—to actually register consciously when you are feeling expansive or when you are contracting and getting small. You begin to connect the dots between your thoughts and your feelings because of what is unmistakably evident in your body, right here and right now. Your body becomes your thought monitor and helps you abort the tendency to follow downward thoughts, jump out of the present into the past or future, get stuck in your mind, and fixate on a problem for hours or even days. With attituning, you can detect the transition from expanded, rising, positive feelings and thoughts to contracted, sinking feelings and thoughts by becoming aware of how it feels in your body. Awareness is the "key in the lock" that gives you the opportunity to change direction, tap into the ascending current, and redirect your energy.

Let's take a closer look at how SET and attituning played a part in Carl's good fortune. By using the SET technique, Carl was able to access body-mind awareness that enhanced his ability to process complex mental and emotional information. He was able to redirect his thoughts, pull out of the downward spin, and act with clarity, confidence, and power. Releasing his stress gave Carl more energy and a wider perspective. This allowed him to take on the challenge he might otherwise have avoided and tackle the problem rather than acquiesce passively. When he accessed WBC, his perspective immediately cleared; thoughts and feelings became reality-based rather than obscured by fearful imaginings and projections. He was able to apply his focus where he actually had some leverage and effectively manage his thoughts, feelings, and actions in the places he didn't.

The type of self-reliance Carl experienced is best built on a solid foundation of bodily awareness. In other words, in order to be self-determining and independent in the fullest sense, we do well to start at the ground level of the body. The SET technique and attituning are dynamic practices that will allow you to do just that. In time, you will actually be able to catch those sinking thoughts before they take hold.

5

Viral Beliefs

The moment we want to believe something, we suddenly see all the arguments for it, and become blind to the arguments against it.

GEORGE BERNARD SHAW

≋ Ladysmith, KwaZulu-Natal, South Africa, 1964 ≋

JOSEPH SHABALALA WAKES up from a recurring dream. His ears are still filled with the sound: a choir singing traditional Zulu music in perfect harmony. This dream has visited him a number of times over the past several months. Joseph's spirit speaks to him, telling him that he and his group will tour worldwide. He wonders, *How can we, as South Africans, ever do this?* His doubts are well founded. Joseph is a black man living under apartheid. He and his relatives— brothers and cousins who have been singing together since they were boys growing up on the farm where Joseph was born—are forbidden many basic human rights, including the freedom to travel.

Despite his doubts, Joseph decides to revive Ezimnyama Ngenkani (the Black Ones), an all-male choral group that he has led since 1960. He names the new group after his home-town, a black ox (the strongest farm animal he knows), and the *mambazo*—which means "axe" in Zulu. Joseph begins to teach this new choir, Ladysmith Black Mambazo, to sing in the perfect harmony he has been hearing in his dreams.

Joseph and the Black Ones had always been good; they captured the unique sound of their time with a special flair. Once they became Ladysmith Black Mambazo and began to sing along the lines inspired by Joseph's dreams, they became unstoppable. The group won nearly every contest they entered in Durban and Johannesburg, until eventually they were banned from competition—although always welcome to perform. Their first album, *Amabutho*, released in 1973, was the first by black musicians in South Africa to go gold. Their subsequent albums went gold, platinum, and double platinum. By then quite famous in their native country, they traveled to Germany for a music festival and tour in 1981. Then in 1985, Paul Simon invited the group to his recording studio in London to collaborate on his *Graceland* album. Ladysmith Black Mambazo joined the *Graceland* tour, and their rise to international prominence was under way. What the voice of the soul had presaged two decades earlier was now a living reality for Joseph and his group.

Like Joseph, many of us have inspirational dreams, inner visions, and innate desires, and yet we *feel* as if something is holding us back. Some inner resistance or reluctance stops us from taking action and getting what we want. The culprit is often a limiting belief like the one Joseph expressed when he questioned, *How can we, as South Africans, ever do this?* His limiting belief prevented him from seeing beyond the immediate obstacle to the field of infinite possibility where apartheid might one day be abolished. Fortunately, Joseph did not stop doing what he loved in the face of what seemed a genuinely solid wall blocking the path to his dream.

Are you as persistent as Joseph? Do you follow your dream when the road ahead is unclear or appears to be riddled with obstacles? Do limiting beliefs stop you from singing your song?

The reality is that the seeds of both success and failure are latent within all of us. Which of these seeds will sprout is truly up to you. Unfortunately, the seeds of failure are invisible to the untrained eye. This chapter will train you to recognize and then discard seeds of failure while sowing and nurturing seeds of success. Let's start by examining the nature of these seeds, which frequently come in the form of *beliefs*.

Your Reality-Making Blueprint

The *Encarta* dictionary defines "belief" as the "acceptance by the mind that something is true or real, often underpinned by an emotional or spiritual sense of certainty." This definition highlights the multidimensional nature of beliefs, which engage all aspects of who you are: mental, emotional, physical, spiritual, to name the most obvious. It is this multidimensional nature of beliefs, and the fact that they live within you on so many levels, that makes them so powerful and so important to understand. When you understand beliefs for what they are, you can begin to "get a grip" on the intricate control panel known as your belief system.

Beliefs are the lens through which you view the world. They can

:: influence your perceptions
:: define for you what is good, bad, true, real, and possible
:: skew your perspective in positive or negative ways
:: direct or limit the actions you take, or both
:: shape your character
:: affect your relationships
:: establish a specific course you will follow

:: determine your health
:: harness or hijack your passion
:: raise or lower your level of happiness.

Each of us lives within and operates out of a complex set of beliefs that define us and the world in which we live. Beliefs are our reality-making blueprint—the way in which we process the flood of information that comes in through our five major sense organs every single moment of every single day. Your beliefs organize the world for you. Without them to help you interpret the massive dose of stimuli that comes at you on a daily basis, you would be overwhelmed the minute you open your eyes in the morning.

That which we *believe to be true* we tend to then perceive and experience as *being true*. We rarely call our beliefs into question, which is why they tend to become self-fulfilling prophecies. As long as beliefs remain unchallenged, they shape your perceptions and direct your actions at a subliminal or subconscious level. Your fate is more or less sealed—or, to be more accurate, your reality-making process is governed by your belief system. Fortunately, each moment holds the potential to break the spell an unconscious belief may have cast over you.

James Allen, author of *As a Man Thinketh*, wrote, "Belief always precedes action." Since your beliefs determine not only if but how you take action, positive beliefs are more likely to foster actions and attitudes that attract positive outcomes. Likewise, negative beliefs are likely to foster attitudes and actions—or inaction, as the case may be—that run contrary to your desires or stated goals. This second scenario is the causal factor for many people whose dreams have yet to materialize.

The fact that we often do not question negative beliefs and simply accept them as *the way things are* makes them particularly noxious. I coined the term *viral belief* to drive this point home. Viral beliefs are similar in many ways to the parasitic viruses that inhabit and occasionally sicken your body. They can be extremely poisonous, yet they can lie dormant until some external factor or emotional trigger causes them to become active again. Viral beliefs can also spread from one person to the next in a highly contagious fashion.

The good news is, no matter what has happened to you in the past, your course is not predetermined. Fate has not left you out in the cold, and the life you desire is just around the corner once you tweak the belief system that governs your reality-making process. Before we launch that particular mission, however, let's take a deeper look at how our beliefs come into existence in the first place.

Who Makes This Stuff Up?

It's not a trick question, although the answer can turn you into a trickster. In the Native American tradition, the trickster is that one who breaks the rules to stir things up for a positive effect. This is the power you gain once you learn how to investigate the who and what that created your beliefs in the first place. Unexamined beliefs operate within you as fairly rigid "rules of reality." Examined beliefs are far more adaptive; they allow you to bend the rules and even change them as reality unfolds.

> *We are all tattooed in our cradles with the beliefs of our tribe; the record may seem superficial, but it is indelible.*
>
> —OLIVER WENDELL HOLMES

Many of your beliefs, positive and negative, are hand-me-downs you inherited from your family, community, and culture. You are conditioned by certain attitudes, mind-sets, and ways of interpreting reality that worked for those who came before. The good news is, your ancestors survived. The bad news is, they may have done so on the basis of partial information or inaccurate points of view. Regardless of their validity, these beliefs are downloaded into you during formative years long before you are able to understand, much less question, them. These are best understood as collective beliefs. You did not make them up, and they are not specific to you, yet they do shape your experience of yourself and "the way life is."

Some collective beliefs are symptomatic of a particular ethnic group, geographic area, historical period, or religion. One example is the notion that the world is flat; belief in "original sin" is another. Some of these inherited beliefs take shape as superstition and govern specific behaviors. For example, I was brought up to believe in two particularly strong assertions that turn out to be utterly untrue: (1) if you step over someone, she or he will not grow, and (2) if you put your shoes anywhere but on the floor, your feet will burn. To this day, the very thought of putting my shoes anywhere but on the floor gives me the willies!

We also have more individualized beliefs that have their genesis in traumatic events. Viral beliefs can be formed when an experience has high-voltage emotional impact and is therefore difficult to fully feel and release at the time. The unprocessed emotional residue remains in the body as somatic memory, emotional stress, energy blocks, and physical tension; these can influence a person on many levels by establishing patterns of thinking and behavior that persist. In this way, past trauma

gets superimposed on the present and is sublii.
enced over and over again

One client was humiliated in front of his commu.
a baseball coach who shouted, "You're worthless!" when ᴜ.
boy struck out. The incident infected the boy with a viral belief
that held: *I'm no good for the team.* This thought got absorbed
into his subjective reality and became defining for him. As
an adult, he had tremendous difficulty whenever required to
present his ideas to a committee or work group.

It is the emotional impact of such experiences that causes
them to take up residence in the body-mind as beliefs about
the world and one's place in it. Such limiting beliefs grow and
mature with us. When we face similar challenges later, the
virus becomes active and dictates how we think, feel, and
behave. Countless incidents in childhood transfer these messages to us at defining moments.

Baltimore, Maryland, 1963

My cousins and I adventure away from our safe, row-house
neighborhood for the first time. We reach the main boulevard,
Park Heights Avenue, full of eager excitement to fly out of
the nest and explore the big outside world. Suddenly a shiny
black car with dazzling silver chrome pulls up beside us. Eight
roughnecks in black leather jackets climb out smacking their
fists together. I'm astonished that so many guys can fit into one
car. They announce themselves as the Bucky Woods gang and
say, "Your kind isn't welcome on our turf." My friends and
I barely escape the attack by racing home, numb and silent
with fear. That incident created a viral belief that influenced
my life for many years: *leaving my safe haven for the wider world
is dangerous.*

Paper Tigers

Among the Chinese, a paper tiger is anything that appears to be very powerful but in reality is nothing to be afraid of —though outwardly a tiger, it is made of paper, unable to withstand the wind and the rain.

Viral beliefs are essentially paper tigers—they are illusory. A paper tiger looks like a tiger, but it can't eat you. If you believe it is real, you will run away. Your body will respond with a biochemical cascade that signals one thing: danger! Your feet will either get you out of there or freeze you in your tracks. Your viral beliefs can have a similar effect. As long as they are unexamined and remain unchallenged, you will live in fear. You may think that some circumstance is standing between you and your goals, when really it's a paper tiger. Your viral beliefs have no bite unless you give them teeth.

One of my clients, Susan, did just that: she *believed* and *lived as though* her opinions weren't important. This viral belief had plagued Susan most of her life. As a result, she was very quiet and had difficulty participating in conversations with friends or interactions at work. She reported feeling unhappy because "people really never get to know me." In our session, she uncovered the roots of this belief. She recalled how her older brother frequently interrupted her when she tried to speak. Her family usually chose to pay attention to him and ignored her. Being impressionable like any child, Susan formed a viral belief that held: *what I have to say must not be important.*

This belief persisted into adulthood and set up numerous subconscious behavior patterns that confirmed and reinforced her conviction. She consistently initiated conversations at inappropriate times. She gave her paper tiger teeth by opening an important discussion with someone whom she knew needed to rush off to a business meeting in a few minutes. Her covert intention, provoked by her viral belief, was to prove that she was unimportant when the person inevitably excused himself. Her behavior was precisely designed to fit this blueprint—why else would she ask her boyfriend a crucial question like "Do you want to go away in November or December for our vacation this year?" moments before the curtain went up at a Broadway play? Her viral belief—*No one listens, and no one really knows me*—had become a self-fulfilling prophecy. Not only did her paper tiger have teeth—it was chasing and biting its tail.

Viral beliefs are buried so deeply in our bodies and our subconscious minds that we may not even know they exist. We accept their truth without questioning the limitations they impose. They become a familiar part of our operating system that we take for granted. Like other viruses, viral beliefs can lay dormant for years and then flare up suddenly when triggered by stressful situations and events. Once again, and this is key, having viral beliefs does not mean you are doomed to a predetermined fate. Whole-body consciousness can help you cut through the illusion of your particular paper tiger and tweak your blueprint so it works in your favor.

San Francisco, California, KRON-TV Green Room, 1992

I am excited as I wait to go on TV to discuss my first book, *Richer Than You Dreamed*. The studio assistant opens the door and says, "You're on in five." All of a sudden, a wave of anxiety shoots through my body. I stand up, relax, and take several deep breaths while making a scan of my body for feelings. I shake and shimmy to release the tension I am feeling. As I do this, I flash on the incident at Park Heights Avenue that occurred when I was thirteen years old. I connect the dots. I am about to step out of the safety of my known world into the wider world of making a television appearance. My body still remembers that earlier danger. I continue to breathe, relax, and access whole-body consciousness. I speak aloud with total conviction: *"As I share my ideas with millions of people, I will be safe."* I feel a pleasurable flood of energy moving through my body as my confidence returns.

The interview went beautifully that day because I was able to get to the source of my anxiety, release that fear, and then choose a more positive outlook. Many of my clients have reported similar anxiety upon being asked to give a speech at the office or a social function. One man traced his fear of public speaking back to the first time he stood up in grammar school; his zipper was down, and the entire class laughed at him. The simple act of standing in front of people would trigger that fear and shame and activate his viral belief: *I'm terrified of getting up in front of people because they will laugh at me.* The paper tiger was still baring its teeth forty years later!

The Enthusiasm Thief

In sessions and seminars, I always ask people what they *really* want in life and invite them to articulate the dreams they would pursue if time and money were not an obstacle. With genuine excitement, they begin to put their heart's desire into words. The dream might be of buying a home, starting a business, finding a mate, writing the great American novel, or scoring a screenplay. Of course, some people have fleshed their dreams out more than others, and some people are more realistic than others. For the purpose of this discussion, "fleshed out" and "realistic" are neither here nor there. What does show up here and, as a consequence, *there*—meaning *in the field of all possibility where our highest dreams lie in wait*—is a subtle form of terror. That may sound strong, and yet I have seen this happen time and time again. A man expresses his dream, and within a matter of seconds, his posture starts to shift, and he shrinks a bit. A woman's face lights up as she puts her deep desire into words; no sooner does the utterance leave her lips than the enthusiasm drains from her face.

What just happened?

A person expands to embrace an imagined larger life and then immediately contracts. This shrinking, pulling-back response is so widespread that we could call it a syndrome. For example, a man might say, "I want to buy a house," or "I want to start my own company." As he expresses his desire, he feels a flood of excitement and energy because he has tapped into his desire. This then triggers a cascade of viral beliefs that get in the way of his fulfilling that desire. That tug of resistance causes a loss of confidence that is linked to feelings of fear and resignation located in his body. He doesn't think any of this through—it just happens. His mouth opens, and out comes a self-defeating statement that begins with "but . . ." and is followed by any one of many reasons why he cannot go after his dream. I call this "I want, but . . ." syndrome the *enthusiasm thief*.

Like annoying pop-up ads on the Internet, the enthusiasm thief jumps onto the screen of your mind uninvited. The enthusiasm thief is held in place by viral beliefs that squelch your excitement by generating excuses, doubts, and "what-ifs." Every time this happens, your positive energy is drained off, and the viral belief is reinforced. Rather than arrest the thief, you give it more of your life power and more power over your life.

Here are some common examples:

I want a new home, **but** I don't deserve it / there's nothing
   affordable.
I want to write a book, **but** no one will read it / it takes
   too much time.
I want to be a singer, **but** I'm not talented enough / I'm
   too old to change careers.
I want a lot of money, **but** it's sinful/selfish to want it /
   I'm not good with money.
I want to be in love, **but** I'm afraid to be hurt again / I'm
   not attractive enough.
I want to start a business, **but** it's too risky / there's too
   much competition.

Do any of those sound familiar? Any gulps or body tinges
while reading them? Later in the chapter you'll have the
opportunity to explore your own "but" statements and put
them away for good. First, I want to share an account of a client
session to show how the enthusiasm thief robbed one man of
his dream . . . until he got wise to it.

Dr. Lou came to me because he wanted to have a successful practice as a chiropractor. He was single, intelligent, well
educated, and had a genuine desire to help people. Practically
speaking, he was doing all the right things: he had launched
a comprehensive marketing campaign, had printed expensive
brochures, and regularly attended networking events. Still,
success eluded him.

Dr. Lou appeared uneasy as we began our first session. His
posture was stiff, his breathing shallow, and he spoke quite
rapidly while his hands made sharp, repetitive gestures. He
was noticeably uncomfortable in his body—an especially loud
"ding" for a chiropractor, who ostensibly hopes to help others

feel at ease in theirs. I began the session by having him stand with his eyes closed, tap into WBC, and declare his self-evident truth.

Dr. L: My chest is very tight, and my shoulders are hunched over. I feel sad . . . *really* sad.

SS: How does it feel to connect to your whole body like this?

Dr. L: Foreign. I feel like I am in my body for the first time in a long while.

SS: Let's take it a bit further. Keep breathing and scanning, and say whatever you notice or feel. Declare your self-evident truth several times in a row. Magnify what you are feeling.

Dr. L: My chest is really tight, [his voice gets louder] and it hurts. My shoulders feel collapsed [his voice starts to shake], and this sadness seems endless.

SS: Are those feelings familiar to you?

Dr. L: Very.

SS: Now tell me what you desire and what you feel. Try saying it like this: I want _____ , and I feel _____ .

Dr. L: I want to have a successful medical practice, and I feel sick and sad.

SS: Repeat that three times, and notice what your body is telling you.

Dr. L (after he repeats it three times): My whole body is buzzing, and I feel very small.

SS: Is that familiar?

Dr. L: Well, the small part feels very familiar.

SS: Do you remember the first time you felt small, sick, and sad like this? Take some deep breaths and listen to whatever your body is saying to you. Tell me if an image appears in your mind's eye.

Dr. L: I see myself as a young boy of six. I am sitting all crunched up near a window.

SS: What are you doing?

Dr. L: I am watching my friends play with the new bikes and skates they got for Christmas. I want to cry because I got nothing.

SS: Why did you get nothing?

Dr. L: Wow . . . I completely forgot about what happened next. My dad came in my room and told me that my friends had rich fathers who made a lot of money. Then he sat down next to me and said, "Son, in order to have all of that stuff, those people work all of the time. They work so hard they get sick. Do you think working that hard and having all of those things makes them happy? No. That kind of success doesn't make people happy. It just makes them sick."

   Pioneer biologists like Candace Pert and Bruce Lipton call what Dr. Lou experienced in this session a *cellular memory*. Our memories, habits, interests, and experiences are stored in all the cells of our body, not just in the brain. These can be triggered into conscious memory under certain circumstances. Connecting to WBC in this way allowed Dr. Lou to access his somatic intelligence and activate the cellular memory held within his body.

The incident seeded a belief in his mind that later bore bad fruit in the form of an unconscious fear that success would make him sick. I encouraged him to bring this unconscious viral belief further into consciousness by speaking it aloud several times: "I want to have a successful practice, but I am afraid I will get sick." As he did this, his body naturally started to move along with the frozen energy that had held the belief in place—in his case, the subtle terror of illness. I had him move his shoulders and chest, shaking them to further release the energy and in so doing, liberate his upper body. He began to feel very alive and free; that decades-old tension was draining away. We then introduced a new belief that embodied his conscious desire to serve others *and* maintain his own excellent health. I had him say the new belief—"Having a successful practice makes me healthy"—aloud three times. At this point, he began to experience some difficulty.

Dr. L: I am having trouble saying it without choking and scrunching up.

SS: That's because your body-mind doesn't believe it yet. Keep saying it and breathe deeply and let your body move instinctively. Your body has carried the belief that success would make you ill for many years, so keep downloading the new message into your system as your body and mind reorganize themselves. In time your whole body and mind will accept this new message as true.

Dr. L (after saying it a few more times and letting his body move instinctively): The more I say it, the less I'm choking and scrunching. My body is getting more comfortable each time I say it.

By the time we completed the session, Dr. Lou had successfully

:: uncovered a viral belief
:: expressed and released frozen emotions that had been an inhibiting force in his body
:: become centered, grounded, relaxed, and revitalized.

He reported that a huge weight had been lifted from his shoulders and left my office standing tall with a big smile on his face.

Not everyone retrieves a clear cellular memory the way Dr. Lou did in this session, but most do report physical and emotional relief. For example, a person might say, "The heaviness I've felt in my chest for ten years is gone," even if they don't experience a cellular memory. WBC activates the latent potential of the body and mind to *work together* and in so doing, to express, release, and change a viral belief even when no specific memory is associated with it.

When a client experiences a memory, I encourage contacting someone, such as a parent, who can corroborate the memory and fill in further details that increase understanding. This encourages a more complete release of the viral belief while making room for new, positive perspectives to take hold. This is what happened for Dr. Lou. After our session, he called his father and asked about the Christmas memory. His father said, "I can't believe you remember that." He explained to Dr. Lou that he'd been experiencing financial problems at the time. He felt ashamed that he couldn't afford to buy presents and made up the story as an explanation. Dr. Lou's father apologized, and the two agreed to set their sights on his success.

Dr. Lou quadrupled his business over the next six weeks. It was an impressive result, and yet small compared to the overall improvement in his day-to-day life that came with having discovered whole-body consciousness. He reported feeling more alive than he had felt in many years. Friends regularly commented on the change. Today his life continues to flourish as he follows his heart's desire. He not only has a thriving medical practice, but he is happily married and has two beautiful children.

Now it's your turn. Take a few moments to consider your own desires and beliefs. Begin by taking several deep breaths and tapping into your self-evident truth. Relax into whole-body consciousness. When you're ready, answer the following questions and notice what you feel.

:: What happens when you dream of something you would like to have in your life?
:: Do you follow through, or do you forget about it or find excuses why you can't create it?
:: How many great goals or dreams have you conceived and then ignored, given up, or not followed through on?
:: Are you aware of a voice or body sensation stopping you from believing you could really get what you want, or taking action?
:: What do you think might be the source of this procrastination or inaction?

Of course it isn't feasible to act on every inspiration that you have. Nonetheless, ask yourself which one or two important visions or goals you have been putting off. Now imagine how your life would change if you stopped putting off your dreams. The balance of this chapter provides specific exercises to help you do just that.

Deeper to Diamonds

There was a South African farmer who purchased a parcel of land. The soil was hard and dry and pitted with rocks. Faced with so many obstacles to growing profitable crops, he quickly became frustrated and gave up. He believed it was not possible to prosper on this land. He decided to cut his losses and sold the farm. The family who bought the farm was very happy to have the land. When they came upon rocks, they did not get frustrated and give up as had the previous owner. Instead, they dug deeper, all the while believing they could turn the soil into rich, soft ground on which to grow crops for food. They saw and appreciated the land's potential and devotedly cared for the soil, believing it would eventually feed them. One day, as the family members worked together digging out an underground stream, the youngest brother found a particularly hard and odd-looking stone. A diamond! In time, the family discovered they had actually bought not a farm but a highly profitable diamond mine.

There are unexpected riches hidden in you, too. If you are willing to dig deep and work through the exercises below, the treasure in your heart can be unearthed.

·························· ⋛ EXERCISE A ⋚ ··························

Identify and Release Viral Beliefs in Seven Steps

1. Get centered. Take three deep, slow belly breaths in and out through your nose. With each exhale, relax your body and let go of any tension. Then, continue to relax. Feel your body. Continue breathing deeply into your belly. Touch your belly with both hands. This step brings your awareness inside, connects you to your body through feeling, and activates whole-body consciousness. Close your eyes, keeping your hands on your belly, and try this a few times.

2. Notice your body sensations and declare them out loud. Notice all sensations in any part of your body. Sensations may include tension or tightness; tingling, vibrating, or twitching; pain or discomfort; a pleasant sense of relaxation; and perhaps even a sensation of heat or cold. Declare your self-evident truth out loud. Describe each sensation: "I notice

_____."

Close your eyes and do this a few times.

3. State your desire. Visualize and feel your desire, the thing you want most in your life. Breathe in deeply through your nose and out through your mouth. As you inhale, imagine that you are breathing the very thing you desire into your whole body. Feel it saturating every cell and being anchored in your body. Now state your desire with total conviction: "I want

_____."

Notice if you feel any hesitation or doubt as you say it. Try to visualize it as you say it. Notice your body sensations again.

Continue breathing in through your nose and out through your mouth. Notice any body sensations that arise from stating your desires. "I notice _____."

Again, you can try it with eyes closed.

4. Declare your desire and state your body sensations at the same time. "I want _____ , and I notice

_____."

5. Repeat, exaggerate, and identify any viral belief that arises. Repeat your desire and say out loud any feelings or thoughts that arise in response. Continue to breathe deeply in and out through your mouth, and concentrate on the sensations in your body. Repeat your desire as a mantra-like affirmation six times or more while letting your body express itself in exaggerated movements. For instance, you may feel tingling in your hands and instinctively shake them, or you may feel moved to wriggle your body, slump in relaxation, or go through any number or series of movements. Exaggerate any movement that occurs to you. Continue breathing, deeply and fully, allowing your instincts and urges to surface spontaneously and be expressed. Make sounds if you wish. Place your fingertips on areas of your body that feel the most sensation, and press lightly on places in your body that have the most sensation. This increases awareness in that area. Express everything that your body wants to express through words, sounds, and movements until you feel done.

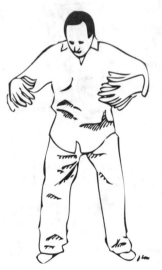

Now, take a relaxing breath and open yourself to any familiar feelings or memories that surface. These may be linked to your desires or your viral beliefs. You may feel an emotion, like anger or sadness or fear. If nothing comes, speak your desire and express your energy or feelings through exaggerated body movements until something does.

You may or may not access a memory or emotion. It doesn't matter. In doing this step, you will release your trapped energy and get in touch with your core self. Whole-body consciousness is profoundly integrative, whether or not you experience a dramatic release the first time you do the exercise. You will most likely feel more relaxed, calm, centered, and aware. Celebrate your gain, whatever it is. The more you practice this exercise, the deeper the results will be.

6. Declare your desire *and* your viral belief or emotion: "I want

_____ , but

_____ "

Repeat this several times, noticing your body sensations, breathing in and out through your mouth. Relax, pay attention, and feel how this feels.

7. Declare your desire, and program your new positive belief or emotion. State the opposite of your viral belief or negative emotion, and replace the word *but* with *and*: "I want _____

_____ , and

_____."

Repeat this several times to begin to integrate the connection and close the gap between what you want and your supportive belief or emotion. Notice how your body is absorbing this new information. It may require a few times or many repetitions for your supportive belief to fully sink in and become embedded in your body-mind. Embody your positive belief and emotions in this way, and you become a magnet for the people, situations, and circumstances that carry you toward your goals.

Embody the Antidote

Following are two techniques that can be used as "anchors" to support you to kick your "buts" out of the way and disentangle your limiting beliefs from your desires.

···················· ≩ EXERCISE B ≩ ····················
Whole-Body Affirmation (also known as Dive Afraid)

IMAGINE YOU are standing before a beautiful pool at the foot of a majestic waterfall. You've heard that this is a popular diving location for brave souls. You experience a sudden desire to climb up the rocks to the top of the waterfall and dive into the crystal waters. Up you climb, and when you reach the top and look down, you are suddenly overcome with fear. Your body freezes. You are now at a choice point. You can climb down and ease your discomfort temporarily, but you don't want to leave with regret and feel disappointed that you didn't jump and vanquish your fear.

The other choice is obvious: you can go ahead and jump. But you're still afraid. The dilemma is the conflict between two opposing emotions, both strong and real. You really *want* to jump. And you're really *afraid* to jump. Is it possible or wise to follow through on your desire even though your emotions are ringing alarm bells? Can you dive afraid? Can you have your desire and feel your uncomfortable feelings at the same time? The answer is yes!

The key is disentangling the two.

To do this, you simply state your desire out loud. In this case, "I want to dive." Then state your fear or viral belief out loud. In this case, "but I'm afraid." You are acknowledging that both are true at this point. They only stay entangled when you are not conscious of them. Becoming conscious separates the two streams of thought.

Separating what you truly desire from the viral belief or strong emotion that opposes your desire is an important step toward achieving your goal. The practice of teasing these two strands apart works for anything. You can apply this when afraid to address a difficult topic with your spouse, talking to your boss about a raise, or approaching your rich uncle for start-up funding for a new business. Most of the time, when you express an "I want," there is a "but . . ." attached to it like an anchor that keeps you from getting anywhere.

Michael had developed a new software program that increased productivity, reliability, and profitability. He had vision, purpose, desire, and a great product. But (there's that word again!) something was holding him back.

In our session, when he voiced his desire aloud, "I want to sell my invention," and then tuned into his body, he was flooded with memories from his school days. As a kid, he'd been known as "Mikey." Always a top student and original thinker, Mikey made the other kids feel insecure and jealous. Whenever he shared a unique idea, his classmates would mock him, saying, "Who do you think you are, Albert Einstein?" Even some of his family members taunted him by calling him a "know-it-all." Wanting to be accepted, Mikey kept his original ideas and his smarts under cover. His fear of being rejected trumped his natural impulse to share his ideas and insights with others. Now he realized that this same fear had become entangled with his desire to succeed in his business venture.

Having connected the dots from the past to see the larger picture in the present, Michael was able to say, "I want to sell my invention . . . but I'm afraid I won't be accepted." He began to disentangle his "want" from his "but . . . ." Now Michael was at a choice point. He could take committed action toward his heart's desire, or he could continue to let his "but . . ." stop him.

Becoming conscious of these divergent intentions empowered him to disarm the enthusiasm thief and dismiss his "but . . . ." He then began to move his "want" forward. This new clarity made him less hesitant and fearful; he became more determined and committed. Within a few weeks, he was enrolling investors into his fledgling company. Today his software invention is selling successfully.

When you feel and acknowledge both your "want" and your "but . . ." you become conscious of your dreams and your obstacles. This allows you to make a choice and act on behalf of your dreams without letting fear stop you. Ultimately, like Dr. Lou, you want to release the "but . . ." altogether. This doesn't always happen overnight, of course. Becoming conscious of fear and acknowledging its roots loosens the grip immediately, however, as was the case with Mike.

························· ≣ EXERCISE C ≣ ·························

Create a Visual Anchor

I LIKE to visualize holding a box in each hand—one contains my desire, and the other contains my fears. This reminds me that I have a choice. It helps me to visualize my desire and my fear as separate entities. It also graphically demonstrates to me that *I* am the one holding *them*, rather than being controlled or bound by them. I like to visualize my desire in my right hand and my fear in my left hand. Then I can turn, look to my left, and consider my fear. And I can look to my right and focus my attention on my desire. I am the one doing the looking; I am the one who has a choice. I am free to choose where I put my attention and to decide which of the two I will follow.

In the next section, you will take what you've learned in the previous chapters and use your brilliant body to re-create every area of your life. Before you turn the page, take a few deep breaths and ponder the menu of opportunities you have; the universe is eager and waiting to deliver your desire.

6

Releasing Trauma

I don't need to manufacture trauma in my life to be creative. I have a big enough reservoir of sadness or emotional trauma to last me.

—STING

There is a healing force hidden in all of us—even if depleted by violence—that is always striving for survival.

—RICHARD MOLLICA, professor of psychology,
Harvard Medical School

⋯⋯⋯⋯ ≋ Baltimore, Maryland, 1957 ≋ ⋯⋯⋯⋯

IMAGINE THAT I am Brooks Robinson—third baseman for the Orioles. I step up to the cardboard box that serves as a makeshift home plate, brush the ground with my right foot, and throw my Pensy Pinky ball up in the air. As the ball comes down, I punch it with all my might. The ball sails over the outfielder's head, but before I even make it to first base, my home run gets interrupted by my mother's voice: "Stevie!"

Punchball is a favorite afternoon sport among the large extended family of cousins and friends that live in my neighborhood. The rules of play are well understood: any player can call time-out when his mom needs something at the store. So I do just that, yelling, "I'll be back in fifteen," and like any errand boy worth his salt, report for duty.

"Go get me a fresh rye loaf and a few half-done pickles from the barrel. Hurry, honey," my mom shouts through the kitchen window.

Feeling exhilarated from the game, I run three city blocks to the store at full speed. Still breathing hard, I dart through the door of Aaron's Grocery. My breath freezes when I see her—Mrs. Margaretten. I can't explain why she makes me so uncomfortable. It's not just that she speaks a foreign language and dresses in funny clothes; there is a mysterious sadness about her. People call her a "refugee," but I don't understand what that means. All I know is that she came to Baltimore from a place called Europe.

Mrs. Margaretten usually wears clothes that cover her arms and legs, but today is one of the hottest days of the summer, and her sleeves are rolled up to her elbows. What I see on her arm makes my stomach turn: the bluish-green number tattoo looks like it was branded into her flesh. Mrs. Margaretten looks over and sees me staring at her arm. Unnerved, I run out of the store and head straight home without the bread and pickles. Half in a panic, I babble to my mother about what I have just seen. She looks uncomfortable and suggests that I go back out and play with the other boys, but I persist. Through a pained expression, she explains what happened to Mrs. Margaretten and other European Jews. I have never even heard the words *Nazi* or *Holocaust* before, much less had I imagined anyone hating or wanting to kill me because of my religion. My mom tells me, "Just forget about it," repeating over and over, "that is what everyone we know has decided to do, just forget about it." But I can see it in her eyes: she hasn't been able to forget.

The Holocaust horror ricochets in my mind: it could happen to her, it could happen to me . . . to my sister . . . my dad . . . to my cousins outside. My whole body starts to tremble. In that moment, my childhood innocence and sense of safety is shaken. The friendly, tight-knit neighborhood where I had always felt so safe and loved was not safe from harm! For the first time, I discovered there was violent hatred in the world, and some of it was directed at people like me. Quite a bit of time would pass before I would realize just how traumatic it was to my seven-year-old eyes and ears to see Mrs. Margaretten's branded-on numbers and hear of concentration camps. That shock lived on in my mind and body as a very real fear and discomfort for years. Even though the event did not involve a direct physical threat or bodily harm, the emotional wound was quite real. My view of myself in relation to people and to the wider world was fundamentally changed.

The dictionary defines *trauma* as "an experience that produces psychological injury or pain" and "a body wound or shock that produces sudden physical injury, as from violence or accident." This chapter explores how *any* mental or physical pain that caused any amount of trauma, no matter how severe or mild, can affect us in our lives today.

Stuck in a Moment

As humans living in bodies, we are vulnerable on many fronts. A threat to any of our basic needs—for sustenance and safety, for love and belonging, for self-esteem and the opportunity to self-actualize—registers on the body-mind as mental, emotional, and physical trauma. Research shows that even relatively common experiences such as the breakup of a love relationship can result in psychological trauma. When unforeseen circumstances bring about a loss of prestige or hope, when we feel betrayed, are humiliated or profoundly disheartened by some course of events, if a nearly realized dream is thwarted or whisked out of reach, we not only feel the stress of that in the moment, we are often left with residual traumatic effects that can impair and even disable us.

In these moments of trauma, we often get paralyzed, like a deer in headlights. You take the hit, your sense of security is shaken, and you are left feeling frightened, helpless, or alone. Overwhelmed, you may freeze or go numb and dissociate from what is happening and how it feels in your body. This numbing affords you some protection and is a natural reaction to an onslaught of intense feeling. However, if your feelings go underground and don't get expressed and resolved, they can play havoc with how you experience the world.

While old wounds are rarely erased completely, I have seen WBC techniques produce a softening effect that loosens the hold of trauma. The frozen moment thaws when we face and release the energy and emotion held hostage in the aftermath of shock. Just as in spring, new vitality and fresh awareness can then be applied to the important next step in the healing process: reevaluating and revising core beliefs—especially those viral beliefs that were formed in reaction to the trauma. I have seen people completely relinquish self-destructive and even addictive behaviors when they resolve old trauma using WBC.

Addiction as Downstream Effect of Trauma

Self-destructive behaviors, including all manner of addictions, are quite often linked to unresolved trauma. From a holistic, body-mind perspective, these maladaptive patterns are easy to understand, even when not so easy to uproot. At the most basic level, what makes an addiction an addiction is the fact that the behavior is not under voluntary control. The impulse to reach for that cigarette, chocolate bar, cup of coffee, or credit card; the urge to call your bookie or buy a plane ticket for one more run in Vegas; and the craving for another shot of whiskey exist beyond your power of self-restraint. Strong urges, cravings, impulses, and dependencies such as these seem to come out of nowhere and take over, even when heartbreaking results are guaranteed. What's wrong with this picture?

In order to see what is happening behind the scenes, we need to connect some very elusive dots. Addictions and self-destructive behaviors rarely pop up out of nowhere. They arise in response to unresolved trauma and are repetitive attempts to avoid and escape lingering pain.

In my work with clients, I have come to see the connection between addictive behaviors and what I have termed "wayward thoughts," as introduced in Chapter 4. Both are repetitive behaviors used to avoid feeling unresolved pain that is stored in the body. From gambling and substance abuse, to compulsive spending, thinking, and talking, to chronic anger, depression, or lateness—all of these behavioral dynamics have hidden payoffs. For example, some people use chronic anger or depression to avoid intimacy or to control relationships. Bottom line: these habitual ploys enable the "user" to avoid feeling difficult feelings. The root addiction underlying all addiction is the compulsive avoidance of feeling—an uncontrollable need to escape the consciousness of fear and pain.

Blind Reenactment of Trauma

When a person carries unresolved trauma in the body-mind, he or she may attempt to resolve it unconsciously by reenact-

ing the trauma in the present. Ty was encouraged to see me by
his girlfriend, Lisa, after an incident that clearly had triggered
unresolved trauma. Prior to when the two started dating, Ty
had lived in a monastery for eight years. During that time, his
days were spent deep in study, meditation, and contempla-
tion. It was a quiet existence; ordinary civilian concerns were
kept at bay by the monastery walls. His reentry into worldly
life involved choices aplenty. Activities that had been off the
menu—such as working for money, finding a place to live,
buying new clothes, even driving a car—were suddenly the
chores du jour. "And then I started dating," he said with a look
of deep concern on his face. "I met Lisa right after I left the
monastery. She keeps telling me that it's only my outsides that
are calm. She thinks I have an anger problem." I offered Ty
the opportunity to explore this for himself using whole-body
consciousness. He was game.

When Ty started breathing and identifying his self-evident
truth, he noticed a lot of tightness in his chest. I noticed that
his fists kept opening and closing. He told me that the anger he
had "tried" to forget during those eight years was as palpable as
the day he first walked through the gates of the monastery. Ty's
mother had been horribly abusive toward him when he was
a small child. It was difficult for him to admit it, but even in
the quiet seclusion of the monastery, he had been haunted by
memories of abuse at her hands. He knew the bodily feelings
that we explored with WBC all too well—the hurt in his heart
and the anger in his fists that wanted to fight back. He could
not fight back against his mother when he was little, and that
pent-up rage was familiar to Ty, as was his resentment toward
women in general. It was one reason he had entered the monastery in the first place—"to get away from *them*."

Midway through the session, Ty stood up and said it felt good sharing this with someone. "I'll be fine now, thanks." I asked him if he wanted to explore his feelings about his mother further. He declined.

Long ago, while watching a television program on reptiles, I learned that snakes shed their skin only when they are ready, and not one moment before. In my years studying and practicing body-centered therapy, I've realized it's quite an apt metaphor for human beings. We don't let go of our old skin—our old way of doing things—until we are good and ready. It was clear that Ty was telling me, *I'm snug in here. . . . think I'll keep this tough old skin of mine.* I strongly recommended he seek help in a men's group or anger-management program and encouraged him to call me if he ever needed to talk. Several months later, Lisa came to see me. Although she had sensed that Ty was an angry man from the beginning and watched his temper get worse week to week, she had hoped he could keep it under control. "But last week he completely lost it," she said. Ty had been arrested and charged with assault. One too many disapproving comments from Lisa, and Ty exploded. "He really crossed the line," she reported. Many of us know—just as Ty did—that we carry past traumas. The key is to address them before our unresolved emotional wounds spill into the present and create havoc.

Up Periscope: How to Manage Submerged Feelings

Using metaphor, we can begin to gain the necessary perspective to work through trauma rather than remain at the mercy of it, as Ty did. Your body-mind is like a submarine, and your inner child lives down inside the ship. This child can't see what's going on up above on the surface of the sea. When some event triggers feelings and memories of unresolved trauma, your inner child confuses it with the past and reacts accordingly. Until, that is, the child realizes that the ship is equipped with a periscope. The adult you—possessed of greater awareness and the ability to witness what is occurring now—is the periscope. It is up to you to alert the hurt child inside and keep him or her apprised as to what is actually happening on the surface. Then you can choose to use WBC techniques and chart a different course—to *deal* with the feelings that were triggered rather than react unconsciously the way Ty did.

Until the later part of the twentieth century, we had little understanding of the precise effects of trauma and the specific mechanism that results in this numbing or freezing effect on the human body and mind. Then came the '90s, the "decade of the brain," which brought innumerable discoveries that revolutionized our understanding of the physiological traces left behind by extraordinarily stressful or shocking experiences. No longer could the psychological community limit its discussion of trauma to those involved in catastrophic circumstances, such as war or natural disaster, or to victims of abuse and violence. Like Ty, we're all susceptible to posttraumatic scars of various depths, and we all have that vulnerable inner child deep within our subconscious.

Neurological Mapping

Threatening events occur all the time, and your body never stops working to anticipate, avoid, and overcome their effects. Your body, as a whole, records and responds to your experiences in specific patterns that "cluster" neurologically. In addition to the cognitive and emotional responses of which you are aware (sometimes to the point of distraction), your body also undergoes a physiological response. Your pulse races, your muscles become tense, and your skeleton contracts—and all of these responses are neurologically "mapped" throughout your body as a memory.

Traumatic experiences are accompanied by a highly charged state of emotion. Specific neuropeptides drop hormones that act as messenger molecules and are released into the body alongside the memory as it is being stored. In a sense, traumatic experiences are placed in storage containers consisting of emotion-linked chemicals in your body and brain. When you get startled or frightened, your body automatically protects itself by secreting a shot of adrenaline, which increases your heart rate and respiratory rate. Your palms begin to sweat. Your pupils and eye muscles go on high alert. Your stomach gets tight, and your digestion shuts down. Your thoughts begin to race. These same physiological responses accompany your reactive response to an event that happens later if it triggers a memory of the earlier, similar circumstance. In Ty's case, his girlfriend's disapproval evoked the helpless child who also remembered the violence that followed that disapproval. His adult self was not so helpless, however, and getting physical with Lisa translated to finally allowing the child within a chance to strike back.

The movie *What the Bleep Do We Know?* features wonderfully illustrative animations that show how the brain confuses what it sees in its environment with past trauma due to the firing of specific neural nets. Dr. Joe Dispenza narrates this segment: "The brain is made up of tiny nerve cells called *neurons*. These neurons have tiny branches that reach out and connect to other neurons to form a neural net. Each place where they connect is incubated into a thought or a memory. Now, the brain builds up all its concepts by the law of associative memory. For example, ideas, thoughts, and feelings are all constructed and interconnected in this neural net, and all have a possible relationship with one another." Later in the film, Dispenza continues:

> We know physiologically that nerve cells that fire together wire together. . . . If you practice something over and over, those nerve cells have a long-term relationship. If you get angry on a daily basis, if you get frustrated on a daily basis, if you suffer on a daily basis, if you give reason for the victimization in your life, you're rewiring and reintegrating that neural net on a daily basis. And that neural net now has a long-term relationship with all those other nerve cells called an "identity." We also know that nerve cells that don't fire together no longer wire together. They lose their long-term relationship because every time we interrupt the thought process that produces a chemical response in the body, those nerve cells that are connected to each other start breaking *the long-term relationship*.

Another explanation for what happened to Ty comes from Arian Sarris. In the book *Healing the Past*, Sarris writes: "Every experience in your life creates neuron pathways inside your brain and central nervous system. The more intense the emotion surrounding an event, the more hormones flood through your body, and the stronger the pathway that is created or reinforced. Every time you recall an event, especially one with an emotional charge, you strengthen that pathway." The solution, according to Sarris, is to alter your memories through change work, "the process of meaningful, focused self-transformation [that] closes off that path and creates another one." He continues, "As you work through your past, you can face the experience of abuse, change the memory to release the poison, and fill yourself with love."

With the perspective provided by Dispenza and Sarris, let's look at two examples of how whole-body consciousness can help us accomplish the interrupt, rewire, and neural pathway rerouting process. First I'll share the story of Leann, a client who wanted to learn to trust men before entering another relationship. Then I will tell you the story of how I followed whole-body consciousness and transformed traumatic feelings held in my own body while visiting Germany and Poland.

The Twilight Zone

Trauma is a fact of life. It does not, however, have to be a life sentence. Not only can trauma be healed, but with appropriate guidance and support, it can be transformative.

—PETER A. LEVINE, *Waking the Tiger*

When Leann and I began our work together, she expressed a desire to get married again. I probed a bit deeper and discovered that she had not been able to deeply trust a man since childhood. In her words, "It's a very subtle anxiety that colors and ultimately destroys every relationship I've ever had." Leann also shared with me that she had felt this anxiety building slowly ever since the birth of her daughter. She sensed there might be some early childhood trauma she couldn't quite reach and had not resolved.

We began with the self-evident truth exercise, and Leann's big toe started to throb. The more she breathed and started to feel into her toe, the more painful it became. Suddenly, to her astonishment and mine, it turned black and blue! I wondered if we'd just entered the twilight zone.

I encouraged Leann to touch her toe, breathe into it, and declare her desire to trust a man. After several declarations, a memory surfaced. She remembered her father dropping her when she was an infant; she had badly bruised her toe. Now in touch with that memory, she shouted out loud, "You dropped me! You don't love me. I don't feel safe with you." In that instant, she understood the source of her uneasiness around men. And she also linked this discovery to why she had often felt nervous when carrying her daughter.

But that wasn't the end of it. After the session, Leann phoned home to check in with her ex-husband. Only moments earlier, their daughter had begun coloring her big toe with black and blue crayons. An event of this kind would be difficult to explain scientifically, and yet nonlocal events such as these are now being explored by leading-edge research. Such an occurrence does bear witness to the complex and intimate ways we are all connected. This connection can serve, support, and heal us. As for connections that limit us, like the unresolved strand of distrust between Leann and her father, those can be unraveled and smoothed out with WBC techniques.

We can avoid unconsciously reenacting old traumas, and we can heal them so as to avoid passing the anxieties on to our children. Leann's breakthrough catapulted her out of a "victim" state into a renewed sense of trust. Within a year she was happily married and expecting a second child.

Often, when people move through a process such as this, they move from hate and resentment into empathy and understanding. Leann reported visiting her dad a week after the session and sharing with him what had happened. This brought them closer and moved their relationship to a richer terrain they had not been able to previously explore.

Getting Unstuck

Your grief for what you've lost lifts a mirror
up to where you're bravely working.

—RUMI

In their book *Trauma in the Body*, Ph.D.s Pat Ogden and Kekuni Minton address the effect of being unable to express the most basic instinctual need of any mammal to defend itself from harm. They point out:

> Trauma calls forth physical defenses such as lifting an arm to avoid a blow, slamming on the brakes in the face of an accident, fighting or running away from an assailant, etc. When such active defenses are impossible or ill advised, they may be replaced by other defenses such as submission, automatic obedience, numbing and freezing. Such less physically active defenses may be the best option in some instances, such as when a victim is unable to fight or outrun an assailant. A victim may instantaneously freeze rather than act, a driver may not have time to execute the impulse to turn the car to avoid impact, or a person may be overpowered when attempting to fight off an assailant. We believe that over time, such interrupted or ineffective physical defensive movement sequences contribute to trauma symptoms.

This information helps us put trauma and its aftershocks in perspective. The body wants and needs to express the active physical defenses we are often forced to override when trauma occurs. If we do this *consciously*, with the intention to calm and reset the nervous system, the unconscious impulse to act out the trauma is relieved. The frozen zones made up of stuck, confused, and disorganized neural nets, with their companion emotional tones and spin thoughts, become accessible to awareness. The light of awareness spreads throughout your body, carrying with it the healing breeze that flows on your breath while you intentionally access WBC. This increased consciousness affords you the clarity and strength needed to reach into the places in your body-mind that still hold the trauma and allow it to run its true course, or at least a truer course than was possible in the presence of the threat. In so doing, you recover what is essential and real—the vital core of your being, your instincts. This, in turn, sets you free to embrace reality more completely and even, in some cases, with great gusto. Until this type of healing takes place, the part of you that wants to say "yes!" to life can be held in abeyance by unresolved trauma. For me, facing unresolved feelings and expressing them through my body meant walking directly into a very dark chapter in recent history and shining the light of full awareness there.

≣ Auschwitz, Poland, April 1997 ≣

A cacophony of whistles and metallic shrieks fills my ears, in stark contrast to the serene farmlands spreading out before me. The wheat fields of Poland evoke a flood of images: cattle cars crowded with people, faces twisted with anguish, arms reaching out from the cars pleading for help, empty trains heading back the other way to herd more families to the death camps. Images like these have haunted me since boyhood. Today I am facing my deepest fear head-on by going directly into the heart of darkness. We chug past an elderly farmer who lifts his head and follows the train with sad eyes. I turn to see his face and watch my own thoughts churn. *He could have been standing on that very spot at his father's side in the early 1940s. They might even have heard the wails and screams of people on the trains. . . . I wonder how his father explained that to his little boy.*

Auschwitz is a mere forty miles west of Krakow in the northeast corner of Poland. Nazi Germany annexed this territory upon defeating Poland in 1939; the first concentration camp was built shortly thereafter. A second site, known as Auschwitz II or Birkenau, was built a half-mile north of the original camp. Auschwitz prisoners were worked to death, literally forced to labor until they perished from exhaustion. Birkenau inmates—mostly women, children, the elderly, and disabled—were simply murdered in cold blood. Ninety percent were of Jewish ancestry. The "Final Solution," as proposed and carried out by the Third Reich, had no precedent in human history; the Nazis had industrialized genocide.

My companion on this odyssey is Gay Hendricks—friend, colleague, and collaborator on the documentary film we are making of the trip. Gay and I have just come from Berlin, where his wife, Kathlyn, has been on a teaching tour for the past two weeks. Kathlyn introduced us to a few of her Berlin students, who then invited us into their homes. There we discovered how the horrors of the Third Reich still weigh heavily on the German people. They too are haunted by the past; they too carry the trauma of the Holocaust in their body-mind.

One German grandmother talked to us about the worst day of her life. She was just a schoolgirl in November of 1938 when Kristallnacht, "the night of broken glass," occurred. Ninety-one Jews were killed in one night, as Nazi storm troopers fueled street rioters into a looting frenzy. Two hundred synagogues and tens of thousands of Jewish-owned shops, businesses, and homes were broken into and robbed or set ablaze.

Between twenty-five and thirty thousand Jews were arrested that night, and systematic deportation to the concentration camps began the next day. "All my Jewish classmates were just gone," the German grandmother reported with a still-frozen look on her face. "And we had to stand and salute the Nazi flag."

We also spoke with the son of a veteran World War II German officer who summed it up by saying, "It's just too big to handle." Like me, Jorg learned about the Holocaust when he was a boy. He has always wondered about his father's activities during the war and feared what part he had played in the atrocities of Hitler's regime. He explained to us that he felt certain *in his body* that his father had participated in the mass murders but could never bring himself to ask the question, "Dad, what exactly did you do?" The cost Jorg pays for not knowing the whole truth is high, and the pat explanation his father always gives when conversation touches on the war—"I never killed any civilians"—wreaks subtle havoc in Jorg's body-mind.

While traveling through Poland, beloved motherland to my father's parents before they fled in the late 1800s, Gay and I are accompanied by an interpreter and guide. Malvina is a college student whose grandmother perished in the Holocaust. While driving from Warsaw across the Polish countryside, Malvina takes us to see an abandoned Jewish cemetery not far from where my grandparents once lived. Located on the outskirts of a tiny village named Karczew, the cemetery has clearly been forgotten. Hebrew-lettered tombstones lie strewn across the ground, overgrown with moss; the forest is rapidly reclaiming the site. While wandering and looking at what remains of this resting place for the departed, I probe the profound sadness I am feeling and drop into the anger just below it. My grandparents left their home when overt civil oppression of the Jews began to escalate. I imagine the pain they must have felt leaving their homeland; at the same time, I feel grateful for their foresight and for protecting our family line by leaving Europe. I reach down and touch one of the headstones, then work to clear a small area of debris and set the stone upright. I am aware that this small physical action is clearing my own body-mind of deeply held sadness. Acknowledging this lifts the weight just enough to allow me to feel and express profound appreciation to my *bubbe* and *zeyde* for their courage. I leave the cemetery sensing that I have just laid claim to the piece of my ancestors' heart that was left behind in Poland.

Later that day we arrive at Birkenau. The darkness surrounding the place is so tangible I fall into a state of shock. Auschwitz II is the most menacing, sinister scene I have ever seen or imagined. Gay is equally appalled and audibly gasps as he takes in our surroundings. Writer and death camp survivor Primo Levi was right when he paid a return visit to Birkenau in the '80s and reported, "Nothing has changed. . . . Rows of wooden barracks intact, its sheer size is terrifying, stretching out as far as one can see."

Gay accompanies me into one of the barracks, where I lie down on a narrow wooden plank. I lie there thinking, *This small ledge served as a bed for up to five men.* The inhumanity of it all is too much for me to grasp. I stretch my awareness to the place below my thoughts, to the knowing that lives in my body, in an effort to understand how and why such profound evil could exist. My body shudders as I begin to grasp at a gut level exactly where I am and what happened here. I feel suffocated by the madness of it all, and my breath constricts into a narrow stream. I am awash in a giant wave of despair. Words come: "I want out of this place, but it's no use." I hear a distant echo and realize that these very words may have been spoken in Yiddish by many held captive in this place. Suddenly, I lose all bodily sensation and retreat to the only safe place left—the depths inside. For several long moments I cannot see a thing. The atmosphere in this place seems to press down on my body. I feel crushed by the weight of overwhelming sadness, by the knowledge of man's unfathomable cruelty to man. Somehow I know the blindness is only temporary, yet I am profoundly disoriented and confused. All I can do is focus on my breath and do my best to stay with my feelings as they arise—riptides of sadness, fear, grief, and rage keep dragging me away from the shore of sanity. Over and over, I mutter, "How could this happen?"

After a while, I open my eyes; my sight has returned. I relax and breathe deeply, tune in to my body, and feel an inner nudge to move. As I start to get up, I once again see and grasp the full impact of where I am. The inner nudge becomes a compelling urge to run, as a new and terrifying animal rage rises inside me. An explosion of adrenaline sends me tearing out of the barracks straight toward a prison watchtower. My instincts are fully realized at last; they bolt through my body. Without a thought, I leap into the air and land a dropkick on the watchtower hard enough to make it crack.

One simple dramatic act—kicking a prison camp watchtower—and I began to feel relief. My body had wanted to strike back for over forty years. Once I had done it—symbolically at least—I began to unclench. All sadness, rage, bitterness, and disbelief began to loosen their subtle stranglehold. As I yelled and screamed, the despair and anguish that had festered inside of me for so long dissipated. I didn't hold back anything. Moments later, I felt my heart open wide as serenity poured in. By feeling and dispersing some of the old anger held in my body, I had created the space to feel something else. Here, in one of the darkest places in history, I was suddenly able to experience some peace.

That night, my last night in Poland, Gay and I went to dinner and a klezmer concert at Ariel's in Krakow. A former *mikvah* (ritual bathhouse), Ariel's is now a Kosher restaurant with a stage and live entertainment. My eyes met those of the dozen or so other Jews who were there. I felt so proud of these courageous people, who continue to celebrate their heritage and rebuild their community amid the blatant anti-Semitism that continues today in Poland. (The *International Herald Tribune* reported that a Jewish cemetery near Warsaw was vandalized the day I left.) A lit Shabbos (Sabbath) candle was clearly visible from any seat in the restaurant. To me, its flame symbolized the hope and possibility that shines through even the darkest shadows. I felt hopeful. I had faced the trauma that had eaten away at me for forty years, brought it to the surface, and released its icy grip through focused action. I dedicated my journey, and the documentary film we made about it, to all of those who never made it out of the camps.

Trauma can be a potent force for spiritual awakening. The inner work we do spreads rapidly to others in society. I've received dozens of letters from people who, upon hearing of my trip to Auschwitz, decided to go on a healing odyssey themselves. Whether a traumatic experience takes you back to Poland, Vietnam, or the home where you grew up, you can follow the lead of WBC to loosen the grip of old trauma on your body and mind. Your choice to wake up to how the past is holding you back and unleash BQ to work through the frozen zones in your psyche is a step toward helping the whole of humanity.

CHAPTER

⋛ 7 ⋚

Discover Your Purpose in a Brand-New Way

Every living organism has a purpose for being here.

—MEHER BABA

You can be anything you want to be, do anything you set out to accomplish if you hold to that desire with singleness of purpose.

—ABRAHAM LINCOLN

·············· ⋛ Baltimore, Maryland, 1949 ⋚ ··············

I N THE FEW short years they have been married, Morris and Tillye have faced and survived every parent's greatest fear: the loss of a child. Baby Howard was only a month old when he died. Four years have passed, their second son is one month old, and their worst nightmare has begun to unfold. Their newborn son has taken ill; he cannot keep his food down. The infant is having periodic convulsions, and the doctor is unable to help. Resigned, he breaks the news to Morris and Tillye: "I'm afraid your son is dying."

Tillye's emotions ride the edge of panic, as her thoughts scramble: *I cannot go through this again.* She looks at her husband with desperate eyes and says, "Call the rabbi."

When Rabbi Liebowitz arrives, he goes immediately to the boy's crib and begins a ceremony.

At birth, the baby boy was named after his uncle and given the Hebrew name Shea. The rabbi decides to perform another naming ceremony and bestows an additional name on little Shea—Chai, which is the Hebrew word for life. Immediately, the infant stops convulsing and grows calm. By afternoon, his fever has passed, and he is able to eat and digest his baby food.

In the close-knit inner city neighborhood where I grew up, my cousins and friends were like one big family. We played together, went to school together, and celebrated holidays together. We liked the same games, ate the same foods, and all wore similar clothes. We were a clan; nobody stood out. So whenever an aunt, uncle, or neighbor would single me out by saying, "Stevie Sisgold . . . what a miracle!" I felt confused. I had no idea what they meant until the day my Aunt Eva leaked a family secret.

"Your mom is sad today," she said. "This is the day your older brother died." I was shocked. I had an older sister, but no one had ever mentioned a brother. When I asked my mom what Aunt Eva meant, she told me about Howard. She told me that she and my father had always hoped for a daughter and a son. I could feel her pain over losing Howard, as well as her awestruck joy at the miracle of my recovery.

Hearing this story at the tender age of twelve affected me deeply. A short time later, I spoke to my Uncle Phil, who had been present when the rabbi came that day. I asked him, "Was it a miracle, Uncle Phil?"

"It was definitely a miracle," he replied. "You were dying. The doctors had given up."

Then he looked in my eyes and said, "I saw you relax the instant Rabbi Liebowitz added Chai to your name that day. Your body stopped shaking immediately. In that moment, you made the most important choice of your life. *You chose to live.* From then on, you were known throughout the neighborhood as the miracle baby. Son, you must have had a good reason to live."

The word *miracle* took on a very tangible and personal meaning after that conversation with my uncle. In time, the notion that we all have a good reason to live—a *purpose* in the truest sense of the word—became a primary focus in my career.

The Miracle of Purpose

That conversation with my uncle planted the seed of a very empowering belief that would later bear fruit. His words opened a window in my awareness and made me alert to each person's innate ability to make choices that produce miracles. That awareness has grown over time and become a cornerstone of how I live and what I impart and *activate* in others.

················ ≩ Thirty Years Later—1979 ≨ ················

It's been two months since I hit the big three-o and left my twenties behind. Something about crossing that threshold has startled me awake; I realize that my cozy life of doing mind-body research, co-owning a juice bar, and growing an enormous amount of organic veggies in the Florida countryside has grown stagnant. I feel an urge for something more. With my family's support, I pack up and head west in search of inspiration and new challenges. I drive and drive, all the way until I reach northern California.

Haight-Ashbury or no Haight-Ashbury, very soon after arriving in San Francisco, I feel the urge to cut my long hair. Freshly shaved, I put on a new Givenchy suit and go out to look for work. It is a glorious day in the city; I would have noticed the breathtaking view of the bay from Embarcadero Center had I not been consumed by spin thoughts. *What am I doing here? I don't know anyone in this town. How am I ever going to make it here? I've got mouths to feed! And Jesse will need college tuition one day.* . . . . I have all but convinced myself that leaving Florida was a horrible mistake and that my impulsive move will be disastrous for my family. I feel as desperate and alone as I have ever felt in my life. I raise my hands to the sky and say out loud, "Why am I here?"

Right then, a warm, calm feeling comes over me. Perhaps it is the California weather, or my sudden surrender to the state they call "beginner's mind"—being content not having all the answers for a change. Whatever the case, I am clearly ripe for a mystical experience, because an inner voice I've never heard before—at least not this loud—begins to echo throughout my body. It says, "You are here to help others." It is a brief moment and yet infinite in its beauty.

All of a sudden the buildings around me, which only moments before looked like cold, unfriendly concrete, are less threatening. I notice the people walking in and out of nearby offices and feel somehow connected to them, as if an invisible thread exists between us. Then the voice continues, "You're here to help others find meaning in their lives." My surface mind says, "Me? You must be crazy!" But another part of me says, "I want to hear more!" I sit down, close my eyes, and begin to take slow, deep breaths and contemplate this whole idea of having a purpose that actually infuses life with meaning. I say aloud, "I'm here to help people find meaning in their lives." Something inside me goes click, almost like a key in the lock, so I repeat the words several times. When I stand up and look around, I feel light and buoyant. I walk toward the Ferry Building and am awestruck by the beautiful view of the Bay Bridge and Treasure Island.

On the long ferry ride back to my hotel room that afternoon, I plan my strategy: I will go into the city the next day and find a sales position. I figure selling is a natural way to meet people and be free from an office schedule, so that my time would be my own. More important, I reconceive the whole idea of being in sales; I'll be working for much more than the paycheck. Sales will be my "legitimate cover" for my real job: talking to people about their purpose.

As I ferried to San Francisco the next day, I looked up at the Golden Gate Bridge and found myself singing. The pure joy that throbbed in my veins was unlike any I'd felt since childhood.

Before day's end, I had landed a position with a major corporation selling business equipment. When I got back that night, I wrote my purpose, "I am here to help others find meaning in their life," on eight-by-eleven-inch sheets of paper and posted them around my hotel room.

I plunged into my new job, a man on a mission, and set up four appointments the first day. By the end of the week I discovered that—even in fast-paced office environments—people loved an opportunity to talk about themselves. Sure, I was offering a great product at a fair price. But more important, I was able to offer people a chance to step into the most important inquiry an individual can engage: "Why am I here?"

At some point on nearly every sales appointment, I engaged my customers on the topic of life's purpose. Rather than pull out a product catalogue and lead with "My company has been around since 1906," I often led with personal inquiries and related to the person in front of me as a very real being with concerns similar to mine.

When I met with the head of the purchasing department for a megacorporation (with a capital *M*) and opened a dialogue about her life's purpose, she immediately came alive. She was thrilled to talk about what really mattered to her and openly shared very personal stories. The next day, she called to thank me, saying, "I want someone I trust to service our offices." She then placed an order for seventy-nine photocopiers. In time, she ordered more than three thousand machines. The commissions on that account alone were enough to pay for my son's college education.

Within my first month on the job, I became the number two sales rep in the western region. I was number one out of five hundred almost every year thereafter and eventually got promoted to national accounts manager. When asked to share my "secret" with other reps, I tried to help them find meaning in their lives and work. A job is just a job until the one doing it morphs into someone guided by a larger purpose.

A Different Kind of Dividend

Having a life purpose not only inspires you, it provides a doorway to connect with others at the essential level. This, in turn, creates natural success. Knowing your purpose—not just in theory but as something real and vital that you feel in your body—is much more than a motivator. It allows you to engage with life full-on to make better decisions, be more effective, and experience real satisfaction. In short, knowing your purpose transforms every endeavor by infusing it with meaning.

I once heard a story about a young animal trainer in India whose elephants were highly prized. Elephants are known to be quite a nuisance in the open-air markets of India. Their big ears flap, and their huge trunks wag back and forth, knocking fruit and vegetables off the stands and sometimes even knocking over vendor stalls. One day, the young animal trainer rode into town atop a regal-looking elephant. The two walked right down the central corridor of the market without knocking so much as a single apple off a cart. When asked how he'd trained the massive beast to walk a straight line, the animal trainer smiled and held up his staff. The people bowed in amazement and honored him by clearing a special place for him at a large feast that evening. The elephant trainer's secret was this: by carefully placing a staff in the elephant's trunk so that the elephant was holding it, the animal naturally walked straight instead of wagging from side to side.

People are not that different from elephants when it comes to walking a straight line. While we don't have big ears and trunks, we do have big appetites and desires that prod and distract us this way and that. One minute you're on task, and the next you're on your cell phone responding to a friend's text message. One year you're working on a new invention, and the next year you're going back to school to get that master's degree. Once you get the degree, you realize that your subconscious agenda was to fulfill your father's ambition for you rather than your ambition for yourself. When we zigzag like this, we only move farther away from our ultimate goals.

Knowing your purpose keeps you on track by helping you choose where to put your focus. Like the staff in the elephant's trunk, it keeps you from meandering and getting knocked about by your hunger for *something* you can't quite put your finger on. Your purpose infuses life with meaning and guides you through each turn in a manner consistent with it.

The Burning Question

Most of us have no problem talking with great enthusiasm about a movie we've just seen or a fabulous restaurant we've discovered. Not so when someone asks, "Why are you here?" or—yikes!—"What is your life purpose?" When it comes to talking about our purpose, vision, and values, many of us tend to shut down. Purpose is a sensitive subject for good reason: it is central to who you are, and revealing it makes most people feel vulnerable. It's your essence that is being exposed, not one of your worldly identities or roles. Does this ring a bell? Do you find yourself raving about the new album you just downloaded but feeling shy when the conversation takes a turn toward your own core values, achievements, aspirations, and goals?

The question *Why am I here?* is universal among humans. At some point, most people stumble into a quest for meaning and purpose above and beyond mere survival. Those who don't often pay a heavy price—because a life without purpose feels empty. Purposelessness is a major contributing factor in depression, a condition more widespread than ever now. Living with no sense of purpose or direction often drives people to an endless thought loop, a constant refrain of *What is the meaning of life? I'm just taking up space! What should I be doing with myself?* And yet, paradoxically, even questions like these are quite purposeful. In the big picture, such questions are a call to your core; they demand to be addressed and will nag you relentlessly until you lock in on your purpose. So if feelings of emptiness and lack of purpose sometimes taunt you, take heart. It's a sure indication that your essence is growing up through the soil of the unconscious and will soon push up a new green shoot.

Ernest Holmes, founder of the Religious Science movement, defines purpose as "determination with incentive." When you discover and align with your purpose, it will clarify and hone every choice you make. Life is suddenly full of certainty when you both *know* and *embody* your purpose.

Crosscurrents, Smoke Screens, Deflections, and Near Misses

When it comes to purpose, spin thoughts take on very specific forms. Some of the most common ones are often instilled in us almost by osmosis—just as a result of living in the world. Consider some of these ways we avoid, disperse, or muddle our thinking when it comes to purpose: "Oh, talking about myself would be bragging." Or, "I don't like to toot my own horn; it isn't attractive." Or, "I've got an artist inside me somewhere, one day I'll set her free." Or, "Who has time to think about purpose? I have bills to pay!" This is perhaps the largest hurdle we have to leap over in order to walk with a clear sense of purpose. Again, take heart, for the hurdle often proves to be no higher than a street curb once you lock on to your purpose.

Take Katrina's experience, for example. In one of my seminars, Katrina revealed, "I'm having a really hard time building my massage practice. Whenever I talk to people about my work, I feel really uncomfortable." I asked Katrina if she felt authentic when she talked about massage. Her response revealed the problem. When she talked about her work, Katrina always focused on what she thought was most appropriate—the type of techniques she had studied and the schools she'd attended. She could give a great rap on the difference between Esalen, Swedish, and deep-tissue massage, but most people didn't have a clue what she was talking about. What they wanted to know was who *she* was; they wanted a human experience, and what they got was a *Wikipedia* experience.

I asked Katrina why she had become a massage therapist in the first place. She shared that her husband had been in a terrible car accident that had crushed almost every bone in his body. She had massaged him regularly while he recovered from his injuries and in doing so discovered that her touch could actually help heal others. I could feel the emotion in her voice as she spoke. Katrina's mistake was in telling people what she thought they wanted to hear rather than simply sharing who she is and what she loves.

I often talk to people who *think* they know what their purpose and contribution to society is but who have very little feeling or passion connected to it. When questioned, these folks often have someone else's aspirations for them tangled up with their own sense of purpose. The subconscious confusion this creates—and the crosscurrents of familial, professional, even spousal expectations—can wreak havoc on self-worth.

Consciously or otherwise, parents tend to have agendas for their children from the moment of conception. These agendas get woven into our sense of personal worth and value. They want a boy rather than a girl, or vice versa. They have dreams for their offspring that may have little or nothing to do with the child's temperament and innate talents and abilities. My parents dreamed that I would one day be a dentist. I heard the exhortation throughout my childhood, "You are going to be a dentist, our own family dentist." They meant well; their hope was that I wouldn't have to work as hard as they did. Like many children, I didn't want to disappoint them. Unfortunately, biology and chemistry classes bored me to tears. When I started college, it was not in premed. I had to reject that cross-purpose and follow my own sense of direction, which led me to focus on communications and psychology.

Can you identify any crosscurrents when it comes to your purpose? Are you fulfilling agendas that others have or have had for you in the past? Do outdated or inaccurate family expectations still influence your decisions? Take a moment to recognize if your parents, spouses, teachers, mentors, bosses, even your own children have figured your purpose out for you. Have you internalized someone else's ambition or point of view on who you are and what you should do?

If you have experienced an internal tug-of-war between someone else's life purpose and your own sense of purpose, you are not alone. Many people struggle with this subconsciously. You can tease apart these various strands by using WBC. Here's how it works—and this one works *beautifully*! Say the truth about this out loud. For example, I would say, "My parents said I should be a dentist, but I am an author, teacher, and performer." You might say, "My advisor told me my purpose is to help others through medicine, but I truly enjoy being a schoolteacher." Notice how your body responds to the self-evident truth exercise in this context and see what you discover.

The other day I received an e-mail from someone who wrote that she loves teenagers and wants to work with them, but her "advisors" informed her that her true purpose is to make a lot of money doing corporate seminars. I wrote back and said it sounded like her head was saying one thing and her heart was saying another. I suggested she get out of her head and state aloud what she feels in her gut is her purpose. Then I suggested she state her cross-purpose out loud while listening to her whole body. She did this and happily reported back that her body seemed to love the idea of working with teens. She wrote me back weeks later, stating that she no longer worries about others' opinions or the money. I assured her that following her heart's desire and living her purpose will bring ample rewards. She said, "I already am getting them by how I feel right now."

Maria, the owner of a pizza restaurant in San Francisco, also discovered the rewards that come with embodying purpose. She had tons of competition in her Market Street location, and it was starting to seriously affect her business. She tried all sorts of marketing techniques: pizzettes (small pizzas), fat-free pizzas, slashing prices, etc. Nothing worked. During the "garden of wisdom" exercise, which you will do later in the chapter, Maria remembered why she had opened the restaurant in the first place. Her dream had been to start a business that would raise money to help people rebuild their lives in the war-torn areas of her native country, Brazil. When I asked Maria how many people she told about her purpose, she said, "Gosh, no one. I can't tell anyone that, it's too intimate." I recommended she follow the lead of her body wisdom and encouraged her to print her purpose right on the menu and to tell people at all the other places where she did business in the neighborhood. Soon after Maria started doing this, her business increased dramatically. People in the neighborhood who were going out for lunch and were in the mood for pizza would say, "Where should we go? Well, there are three choices. Why don't we go to that restaurant with the woman who supports her people back in Brazil?"

John, a bank vice president, came to one of my men's retreat weekends. The vice president of a bank, John had fallen into the humdrum routine of going to work every day and grumbling at his coworkers until he went home. When he did my WBC purpose inquiry, John reconnected with the real reason he'd become a manager in the first place: to be a leader. He remembered that his purpose was to bring people together and create a strong team environment. He essentially got his "elephant staff" back, and the effect was remarkable. He started to enjoy going to work and arrived full of eager anticipation every day. The atmosphere at the bank grew more convivial and productive once he encouraged his staff to clarify their respective purposes and share them with coworkers. Within two months, his department increased productivity and reduced employee absenteeism considerably. This stuff works! When we realign with and embody our purpose, our motivations change, and our actions reflect more positive results. We then have a much better chance to move toward our dreams with passion, rather than away from the past with fear and dread.

A Life Filled with Passion

Reclaiming a valuable aspect of who you are that was discouraged or denigrated in the past is a surefire way to restore passion, power, and confidence. It may be that your creativity was aborted, your sensuality disparaged, your sense of humor censored. Each of us has something unique and valuable to contribute, yet circumstances sometimes conspire to have us forget or deny that. One remark from a frustrated coach, teacher, or parent can damage a child's spirit and belief in his or her talent. The wound festers, and we carry a doubt about our value in our body wherever we go. Losing our childhood spunk and innate belief in our value holds us back from creative expression.

When our self-regard is low, we get hurt easily if someone doesn't love us the way we want or praise our product, service, or artistic creation. A single, isolated rejection can sometimes be enough to trash a brilliant vision or idea that could have become a great reality. While many of us have suffered wounds to our self-esteem, there are wonderful examples of those who reclaimed their value and found ways to achieve greatness nonetheless; persistent individuals who persevered no matter what anyone said about them or their cause illuminate our history books.

If Gandhi didn't believe in the value of his cause, he would have given up the first time the British regime refused his request for a free India. Rosa Parks's refusal to move to the back of a bus led to the disintegration of institutionalized segregation. On a more commercial level, Sylvester Stallone pitched his original *Rocky* with himself as the star, and it got rejected many times. He stuck to his principles, never stopped insisting that he had to be Rocky, and a great movie was eventually made. Spike Lee financed his first film on credit cards. Even L. Frank Baum's manuscript "The Emerald City" (you know it as the book *The Wonderful Wizard of Oz*) was rejected by several dozen publishers.

We don't like their sound, and guitar music is on the way out.

—DECCA RECORDING COMPANY, rejecting the Beatles, 1962

Pablo Picasso said, "Every child is an artist. The problem is how to remain an artist once he grows up." There's a telling story in that vein, about a psychologist interviewing young children. He asked a classroom full of four-year-olds, "Who here is an artist, a singer, a dancer?" Every child in the room responded enthusiastically, "I am!" In contrast, when sixteen-year-olds were asked the same questions, only a small number of them responded affirmatively. Their innate creative spirit had been squelched.

When I shared that story at a seminar, Daniel, age forty-five, raised his hand. The story brought to mind something that happened to him in kindergarten: "As a boy I loved to draw, and I was very good at it. In fact, I was *so* good that my teacher accused me of tracing. She didn't believe me when I told her I had done my drawings freehand. She made me sit in the corner and wear a dunce cap all afternoon." Daniel threw away his pencils after that humiliation. He hadn't drawn in forty years, even though he still felt passionate about art. During the seminar, he made a commitment to purchase art materials and start drawing again. Six weeks later, he told me that he was drawing and enjoying it as a hobby. He realized that although drawing was not going to be his primary career, it fostered creativity and passion that enhanced his business and personal relationships.

That child lives on within us all, and that child still believes he or she can do anything. What a wonderful, valuable quality to have as an adult! Unfortunately, throughout our lives, most of us have not been encouraged to let that child come out and play. Instead, we buried some of our innate talents and abilities. Fortunately, the potential remains and, once released, can transform our working lives into the playground we long for.

Reclaim any aspect of yourself that was not allowed free expression in the past—your creativity, sensuality, humor, whatever—and passion, power, and confidence will be restored. Your life will take on a new luster and dimension.

Kim was a thirty-nine-year-old graphic artist with enormous creative talent, but she hadn't attracted enough clients to support herself. During our session, she recalled how her artistic talents had been discouraged by her parents, who insisted they had no value in "the real world." Now as an adult, she had difficulty acknowledging that she deserved to be well paid for her extraordinary creativity.

Kim showed me a proposal and presentation package she was about to take to a client. When I asked how much money she was going to ask for, Kim responded in a faint voice with a big question mark, "Five hundred dollars?" I encouraged her to recite her value over and over and let any feelings that wanted to come to the surface. After expressing feelings for an hour and "emptying her tank" a bit, she suddenly said in a strong voice, "I am extremely talented." Her body relaxed, offering no further resistance. She repeated this from the time she left my house until she met with the client. At the conclusion of her presentation, Kim asked for two thousand dollars. "Is that all?" the client said. "I thought you were going to ask for at least five." The client immediately wrote Kim a check. Since then, Kim has quadrupled her fee.

················ ≋ EXERCISE ≋ ················

Your Garden of Wisdom

THE FOLLOWING exercise is a guided process that can help you discover and clarify your life purpose by evoking images that are profoundly personal messages from your unconscious. There are three ways to do this; each works well.

- ⠶ Close your eyes after you read each instruction or question, then open them and write down your response below.
- ⠶ Record this exercise for yourself using the following script, or you can order an audio CD on www.onedream.com. Either way, listen to the entire exercise, and write later.
- ⠶ Alternatively, you can have a friend read the exercise and write down your responses.

Let's begin.

1. **Get SET.** Take a few belly breaths, breathing way down to fill the bowl of your pelvis with breath. Notice your self-evident truth in this moment. Notice your posture. Notice any tension in your body. Notice

your breath. Say your self-evident truth silently to yourself or out loud. For instance, "I am relaxed in my belly," or "I am crunched up in bed, and my neck hurts." Scan again from head to toe. If any area of your body is not comfortable and relaxed, acknowledge that. Take a few more deep breaths into your belly and relax any tension on the exhalation. Breathe tranquility into every pore of your body. Observe any distraction that prevents you from feeling peace throughout your body.

2. **Visualize.** Now imagine yourself in a familiar and safe environment, perhaps on your favorite beach or walking along a trail in the woods. You might even see yourself simply relaxing in the sanctuary of your own home. Notice what good feelings arise as you picture yourself in this setting and breathe this feeling into a specific place in your body. Choose a place in your body that feels like your power center; it might be below your naval—the place martial artists know as the *dantien*—or it could be your heart, your third-eye center, even your hands or the soles of your feet. We will now name this nurturing place in your body your "garden of wisdom." You will visit this place again and again to access your inward knowing, so choose a place in your body you can focus on comfortably. Remember to breathe in slowly through your nose and out slowly through your mouth, relaxing your jaw as you do so. Witness any sensations you feel throughout the process. Breathe all of these sensations into your body.

3. **Inquire within.** After you read or hear each of the following questions, close your eyes and listen inwardly for an answer. Then, open your eyes and write down the first thought, symbol, or picture that comes to mind. Stay open and curious. The words, images, and sounds that come may surprise you.

Repeat this process for each question, one at a time. Remember to breathe in as you read the question, then close your eyes and breathe out. Continue breathing, and wait until something comes; then open your eyes and note or draw it. Then take a moment to scan your body

and notice your self-evident truth once again, saying it aloud. Then
repeat the process.

What is my purpose for being here on the Earth right now? _____
_____
_____
_____

What is uniquely valuable about me? _____
_____
_____
_____

What talents do I have? _____
_____
_____
_____

What are my special qualities? _____
_____
_____
_____

What do I do that serves and helps others? _____
_____
_____
_____

How, when, and where do I get to express my purpose in my career?
_____
_____
_____

How, when, and where do I best express my purpose in my relationships? _____

_____

_____

_____

How can I best express my purpose in other areas of my life? _____

_____

_____

_____

Where in my life am I aligned with my purpose? _____

_____

_____

_____

Where in my life am I not aligned with my purpose? _____

_____

_____

_____

What actions can I take to be aligned with my purpose? _____

_____

_____

_____

Show me a vision of what I look like living 100 percent in my purpose.

_____

_____

_____

Congratulations for taking the time to explore these crucial questions. Take a little time to digest and integrate the experience. Witness and feel what just happened. What did you discover? Perhaps you felt a place in yourself that wants to make a deeper commitment to being a loving person. Maybe a new idea for your business career came to mind. Or you may have received a clear message to make a big change in your life. Taking action comes later. For now, just notice the messages coming from your body.

You can keep the "garden of wisdom" experience alive by looking over the answers and distilling them into a purpose statement that you then post as a daily reminder. Don't worry if your purpose doesn't feel fully baked yet. You can repeat this exercise often. Life has a way of helping you refine and clarify your purpose once you engage the inquiry and bring your whole body to the table.

I yam what I yam.

—POPEYE

·························· ≩ EXERCISE ≨ ··························
A Whole-Body Affirmation

THIS EXERCISE is designed to help you reclaim and embody your value. Begin by creating an affirmation using three specific word commands—*love, accept,* and *express*—before your purpose statement. Use the provisional statement that emerged from your "garden of wisdom." For example, Kim's affirmation is "I love, accept, and express myself as a powerful, creative, and abundant woman who helps others through graphic arts and Web design."

Fill out your own whole-body value affirmation.

I love, accept, and express myself as a _____ (man or woman)
who _____
_____

As you repeat your affirmation, use SET and focus specifically on where in your body you feel any difficulty or resistance to loving, accepting, or expressing your value in this way. Stay focused on that area, and repeat your affirmation until you anchor the new belief in your body.

The words *love*, *accept*, and *express* are more than intellectual concepts or emotional experiences in this context. They are commands that actually activate your subconscious mind and alert it to your conscious intention. You might even learn a good deal about yourself by looking within to see if any of these three words—*love*, *accept*, or *express*—triggers resistance or reaction from your body. For example, let's say you want to succeed as a dancer. You may be able to love yourself as a dancer and even expertly express yourself as a dancer. But when you say, "I accept myself as a dancer," part of you may shout, "No way!" Your gut may grip in a hard, little ball full of the worst kind of butterflies. That's a sure sign that you have yet to fully accept that dance is your call to greatness or, at least, your ticket to great happiness and personal fulfillment.

Notice how your body responds to each component of the formula? Try them one by one.

I love myself as _____

_____

_____

_____.

I accept myself as _____

_____

_____

_____.

I express myself as _____

_____

_____

_____.

Oftentimes a person will reclaim and embody his or her value with this affirmation but find it difficult to hold onto that value in the presence of certain others. Try adding the following:

I love, accept, and express myself as _____ especially in the presence of _____

_____

_____

_____.

Fill in the name or names of whoever intimidates you, makes you squirm, or convinces you that you don't have value.

Value is sewn into the very fabric of your being and never leaves no matter who you are with, what you do or don't accomplish, how you look, how much money you make, or what kind of car you drive. Value is an absolute. Here's a creative exercise to help you keep your eye on the prize.

Take a piece of paper and draw a line with a crayon or marker, dividing it in half. Tune in to how you look and feel when you are aligned with your purpose. Breathe deeply, practice SET, and draw whatever inspiration comes out of you on one half of the page. Be as artistic as you like using paints, pastel crayons, glitter, or art materials of your choice. Then after you are finished, tune in to how you look and feel when you are not living in purpose. Breathe deeply, practice SET, and draw whatever comes out of you on the second half of the page.

Hang or frame your split-screen picture to remind you of the two choices you always have.

Vantage Points and Emergents

According to *Wikipedia* (August 2008), *emergent evolution* is "the hypothesis that, in the course of evolution, some entirely new properties, such as life and consciousness, appear at certain critical points, usually because of an unpredictable rearrangement of the already existing entities." This concept is reflected in systems theory, complexity theory, and chaos theory. When considering life purpose, it's essential to leave room for the inevitable *emergent* element—that unpredictable rearrangement—that life throws our way.

Prior to my trip to Germany and Poland, I had not imagined becoming a documentary filmmaker or having my film influence others to trace and heal their own traumas from the past.

Throughout time and in all parts of the world, humans have given birth to new forms when catastrophe presents us with the opportunity. Consider the heartbreak endured by John and Revè Walsh over the kidnapping and murder of their son Adam. John became an activist in the wake of their loss, and his advocacy eventually led to the formation of the National Center for Missing and Exploited Children. Walsh also became the host of the popular television show "America's Most Wanted"—an emergent that arose as a result of national media attention to Adam's murder.

Auspicious circumstances can be just as catalytic as catastrophic ones. Each step along life's meandering course provides a unique vantage point. Discovering your life purpose is not a one-time event. Continual growth and expansion is the name of the game, and whole-body consciousness allows you to play that game with a more complete sense of who you are and where you're headed.

8

Boost Your Relationship Mojo

A relationship, I think, is like a shark, you know?
It has to constantly move forward or it dies.

—WOODY ALLEN, *Annie Hall*

You've got to know who you are, to know somebody else. You've got to
feel what you feel, to feel somebody else. That's the knowledge of love.

—STEVE SISGOLD, from the album *Know It, Show It*

O Y VEY!
I've been waiting for a full seven chapters to say that!
The literal translation of this Yiddish expression is "oh, woe,"
but its more common meaning is "oh, no!" As I said in the
Introduction, *life in a body is a thrilling adventure.* Few aspects of
that adventure trigger "oh, no!" more often than our interactions with other humans. Think about the last time you
climbed onto a roller coaster and sucked in your breath at the
crest of that colossal slide into elation. Fortunately, on the
truly wild ride of a relationship, whole-body consciousness
can help you keep breathing and turn many a "no" into a
wholehearted "yes!"

Along with books about how to make money and be a success, books about how to have a happy relationship and communicate effectively sell by the gazillions worldwide. We see titles on how to improve love relationships, titles on how to talk to your kids, and titles on how to communicate effectively on a professional level. Our hunger for knowledge in this area is understandable, for our happiness has everything to do with healthy relationships. So what can I possibly tell you in one chapter that you haven't already read or tried? Plenty. More to the point, your body can tell you plenty, as you will see. Your body is your key ally when you want to boost your relationship mojo.

I Got My Mojo Workin' . . .

You've probably heard the word *mojo* used in reference to virility, as in the Muddy Waters song with that immortal lyric, "I got my mojo workin'." Younger generations may recall the film *Austin Powers: The Spy Who Shagged Me*, wherein the spoof-hero loses his "mojo" while in bed with Ivana Humpalot. So, to many of us who learned about this word through pop culture, we think of our mojo as our sexual power. Yet in truth, it means a lot more than that.

Although the word *mojo* is defined often as a type of magical charm, its origins can be traced to the African Congo, where *moyo* means "soul" or "life force." Another curious connotation of the word comes from Hunter S. Thompson, the American "gonzo" journalist and author best known for *Fear and Loathing in Las Vegas*. Thompson used the expression "mojo wire" in reference to the telefax machine, which he considered the highest form of human communication back in 1972. Variant usages and subtle connotations aside, in general usage, *mojo* also means that special spark of creative energy between two people. In this chapter, you will discover a very special "mojo wire"—one that you can verify to be among the highest forms of human communication in your own experience. I call this whole-body communication system "straight talk." A radical departure from the way many of us have been trained to censor our speaking, straight talk allows us to continually refresh the vitality in relationships and turn that spark of energy into fully engaged thinking and relating.

How Do We Lose Our Mojo?

What angers us in another person is more often than not an unhealed aspect of ourselves. If we had already resolved that particular issue, we would not be irritated by its reflection back to us.

—SIMON PETER FULLER, *Rising Out of Chaos*

From a whole-body-consciousness perspective, nearly every relationship conflict boils down to one thing—loss of mojo. How unfortunate it is that over time people often lose the spark that existed between them, and their relationship grows habitual and stale. What causes us to repeat the patterns that degrade our relationships over and over again? Let's turn once again to Dr. Joe Dispenza to help us understand how these unfulfilling relationship behaviors get activated in our body-mind.

In the movie *What the Bleep Do We Know?*, Dr. Dispenza lays out not only the "how" but the "what" of our neurological landscape in respect to relational patterns. For instance, he asserts the following:

Some people have love connected to disappointment. When they think about love, they experience the memory of pain, sorrow, anger, and even rage. Rage may be linked to hurt, which may be linked to a person, which

then is connected back to love. We know physiologically that nerve cells that fire together wire together. If
you practice something over and over, those nerve cells
have a long-term relationship. If you get angry on a daily
basis, if you get frustrated on a daily basis, if you suffer
on a daily basis, if you give reason for the victimization
in your life, you're rewiring and reintegrating that neural
net on a daily basis. And that neural net now has a long-
term relationship with all those other nerve cells called
an "identity."

Here is an example of how this type of "wiring" plays out
in real time. Angie and Tony are a couple who came to one of
my workshops. They were clearly in love, but their generally
good marriage had recently come under serious strain. Both
were feeling burdened and confused by recurring clashes that
occurred late at night. After their most recent blowup, Angie
started sleeping in the guest room, which prompted Tony to
use "the D-word" (*divorce*) for the first time. Neither of them
understood how or why the late-night fights had escalated to
cause this rift between them. I asked Angie to tell me about the
most recent incident. Through tears, she explained:

> It was nothing, really. He'd gone out after work for a
> couple beers and come home late. I don't mind that so
> much; I want him to feel free to spend time with his
> friends, and I like having an evening to myself. But when
> he crawled into bed and kissed me on the cheek, I felt
> repulsed. For a long time, I thought the best thing to do
> was just not talk about it, but it got worse. Then I started
> nagging at him about any dumb thing, and in no time
> I went totally ballistic. Over nothing, really. And this
> has been happening almost every week for the past few
> months!

I asked Angie if she would be willing to tap into WBC to uncover the hot button that causes her to "go ballistic." As she breathed into her body and tuned into my question, a long-repressed memory came to the surface. Angie's father was not a drinking man, but one night when she was twelve, he came into her room smelling of beer. He woke Angie out of a sound sleep just to tell her how much he loved her. Then he kissed her in a strange way on the lips that made her feel very uncomfortable. "The smell of beer reminds me of that night. I felt so afraid, overwhelmed, and even overpowered by my dad's affection. That's why I freak out; it's not you or the fact that you've been out with the boys—it's the smell of beer and the kiss." This recognition dispelled the intense polarity between the two of them. Tony vowed to adopt the habit of brushing his teeth and rinsing with mouthwash before getting in bed with Angie whenever he'd had even a single swig of beer. Tony's concern and understanding gave Angie the signal that she was truly cared for. This joint realization—along with a bit of mint-flavored mouthwash—put their floundering marriage back on solid footing. Their mojo started risin' again.

Another example is Stan and Barb, whose main concern was their sex life; it had become a dead zone. The couple had endured many grueling sessions of talk therapy with no success. I let them know that they would talk in this session too, but not from their heads. I asked them to stand and face each other about six feet apart, and I coached them through the "self-evident truth" exercise. They each spoke their truth aloud while maintaining steady eye contact. I then had them take turns moving closer and then farther away while the other stood still. (Investigating the effect of a shift in the distance between two people is often quite revealing.) The breakthrough came when Stan moved closer to Barb and, rather than speak his self-evident truth, he said, "I notice how closed you are to me sexually." As he spoke these words, his body said something his mind could not say by bringing his hands forward to cover his crotch! So unconscious was this gesture of shielding his groin that Stan would not believe he had done it until he saw a video replay of the session. The video footage spoke volumes: Stan's assumption that Barb closed down whenever he approached her was a projection straight out of his subconscious. He was the one who became protective whenever he drew near to his wife. Facing this brought up an early memory for Stan—a time when he couldn't rise to the occasion in bed with his first crush, whom he had pursued for a year. He not only lost his mojo that night but his first love as well. Stan had long since pushed this incident to the back of his mind, where it stayed—except when he unconsciously projected it onto Barb.

In light of this new awareness, I assisted Stan in revising his self-evident truth statement. With a bit of trepidation, he looked Barb in the eye and said, "As I get closer to you, I notice I am afraid, and I shut down sexually." I asked him to repeat this several times and allow the associated feelings to express fully through his body. As he did this, Barb noticeably relaxed, and tears began streaming down her cheeks. Stan's tears were not far behind. When they returned the following week, Barb reported that she now felt safe enough to open up to Stan. Once he stopped hoisting all that blame in her direction, she was able to let her defenses down and relax. Meanwhile, Stan's ability to "own his stuff" and look honestly at this sensitive issue rekindled her respect for him. They had become lovers again for the first time in years. Stan reported, "I was so consumed by my fear of not performing well in bed that I couldn't even see what was causing me to shut down." Barb added, "It wasn't low libido that kept me from getting turned on; it was the blame he'd been launching at me for our tepid sex life.

Now that all that muddled, unspoken stuff is out of the way, we're hot for each other again!" Taking stock of what was happening both *in the moment* and *in the body* helped Stan and Barb get their mojo back.

Bridging the Gaps

My work with couples over the years has convinced me that any two people can connect on any combination of levels. Let's face it: some people form relationships in which the mojo works on all fronts, while other pairs have it going on in some areas but not others. Couples that connect on all levels not only share common values, interests, and goals, but they are also intellectually compatible, emotionally suited to one another in terms of basic temperament, and physically connected with zingy chemistry. On the other hand, some couples have a fantastic intellectual connection that flows easily, but they are physically disconnected and show little affection toward each other. Some have a strong spiritual connection but no sexual chemistry. Still others have great sexual chemistry but few shared values or visions. And for many couples, the whole question of purpose—both individually and as a couple—is often left unaddressed.

Silence Is *Not* Always Golden

Relationships wherein couples only connect on certain levels can work—if the couple are conscious of why they are together and are content with what they do have. Couples can use WBC to help them recognize and speak consciously about their gaps. The goal is not to force a connection where there isn't one but to bridge the gaps that exist and fill them with awareness rather than resentment. What if we could tell the truth about our differences instead of hurting each other with them? One of the many pitfalls I've watched couples stumble into repeatedly is a tendency to propagate negative spin thoughts and turn them into stories, such as "he doesn't meet me on an intellectual level," or, "she isn't as affectionate as I am."

We all tend to create stories in our heads that are full of assumptions about our partner's feelings and behavior. These stories often have little to do with reality and usually only serve to make us sad, angry, or scared. We then react to these unhappy stories with a "fight or flight" response and either attack, blame, or pull away. This leads to an escalation of problems instead of resolution. Even the healthiest of loving relationships hits a rough spot on occasion. What makes for a healthy relationship is not the absence of challenges but two people who have the needed skills to resolve conflict and work through differences that naturally arise. It can be infuriating to discover that the person you feel the closest to in the world is so different from you in so many ways. Partners in a healthy relationship come to appreciate differences rather than resist them or refuse to accept the other person for who they are.

The Eyes Have It

The following exercise allows you to move away from unconscious blaming positions and, instead, to learn to understand each other better. If you are doing this exercise as a couple, it can help both of you reframe the stories you have made up about each other. If you are single and interested in having a relationship, I recommend you also do this exercise and tune into what you feel when you read this. This will help you discover what areas in your body-mind get triggered in intimate relationships. If you have a partner who would rather walk on hot coals than do a communication exercise, then you might want to explore your self-evident truth about that fact.

Place two chairs in an open area, and sit approximately two feet apart. Look into each other's eyes. (Many couples report that they haven't looked into each other's eyes since courtship.) Take several long, slow, deep breaths while maintaining a soft gaze. Continue doing this and tell each other any self-evident truth that you notice; this will get you out of your heads and into your bodies. This type of sharing is foundational to intimacy; we get close through knowing what another is experiencing. Next, read the list below and take each aspect of your lives together one at a time, and share what you notice in your body-mind as you share. For instance, when you share your intellectual connection, you might say, "When I look in your eyes, I notice that my chest feels tight and that I feel sad that we never have stimulating intellectual conversations anymore." Or in the emotional arena, you might say something to this effect: "As I look in your eyes, I notice my heart beats faster and softens as I know how much you love me and show me that all the time." Or in the spiritual arena, you might say, "When I look in your eyes, I notice I am angry that we don't have any spirituality in our life like we did when we first dated." Or around sexuality, "I notice when I look in your eyes how attracted I am to you, yet for some reason, I feel shut down sexually." Or, "I notice when I look in your eyes, I feel afraid, as I experience that our goals and purpose in being together have vanished."

Tell each other what you feel about your present connection in the following areas, one at a time, and don't forget to practice SET as demonstrated above:

- Intellectually
- Emotionally

:: Spiritually
:: Physically
:: Socially
:: Financially

Another area to discuss with your partner is your purpose and visions both as separate individuals and as a couple. I often have couples do the above exercise with eye-gazing to cocreate a purpose statement for their relationship. This then can be pasted up on an altar in the home and embodied in much the same way presented in the previous chapter.

Polarity Relationships

When we take a position in any relationship, we risk getting locked into a "fixed" image of self and other that can get stuck. This type of polarized relationship dynamic is quite common. A *polarity* is any situation in which two individuals or groups have qualities, ideas, or values that are diametrically opposed to each other. In many a romance, marriage, or business partnership, this dynamic becomes the dominant theme. For example, if I have you "fixed" as smarter than me, I may always feel less smart around you. Two people who spend lots of time together can easily become stuck in their respective roles and find it difficult to get out of them. Viral beliefs that hark back to our earliest formative relationships create these polarity dynamics.

When we relate to others and ourselves in key relationships through the lens of a viral belief, we become trapped by a fixed image of ourselves that limits our potential. When we see the world as big or powerful, we stay small or weak, and so forth. This viral belief runs our lives by creating polarity relationships that reproduce the painful and limiting dynamics of the original unresolved relationship.

For instance, Paul is a watercolor artist whose father told him that to pursue art as a profession would be a waste. He heard this refrain repeated for dozens of years. Not only did this affect his art, but the negativity  leaked into other relationships, too. His father's voice still rings in his ears daily and keeps him from selling his paintings. Bad reviews are a fact of every artist's life, but Paul had let one critic stop him dead in his tracks. He was trapped in a polarity relationship. I told him in a session, "As long you keep your dad as your judge, you will always remain the one being judged. Give him the Donald Trump treatment today: fire him or resign. Only then can you create a new relationship with him and let the world at large be your art critic." Once he expressed and released the feelings that kept him locked in to his father's critique, he began to feel more confident about sharing his art. A few months after he gave his dad the pink slip as his art critic, he placed several paintings in a prestigious gallery.

It is essential for you to identify and change any polarity relationships that may be diminishing your mojo at this time. Consider the following questions carefully:

:: Are you in any polarity relationships that need to change?
:: Who can you release from the position of judge, abuser, know-it-all, etc.?
:: Are there any specific actions or steps that you want to commit to right now? For instance, "I will call my older sister by Friday to talk about our relationship dynamic."

Choice Points

Any fool can criticize, condemn, and complain, but it takes char-acter and self-control to be understanding and forgiving.

—BENJAMIN FRANKLIN

Another navigation skill that really opens the door to con-flict resolution is the ability to understand why and how to drop that age-old relationship demon, *blame*. What makes blame the biggest, baddest form of spin-thinking is its pow-erful allure. When blame arises, it is abetted by our physi-ological response, which is to become quite animated when we feel threatened. In every interaction we have, there is always a choice point, and blame is *never* a good choice. WBC allows you to recognize what is occurring in the moment at a physical level, where blame is fairly easy to recognize. Think about it—or better yet, *feel it*. Feel the finger-pointing energy and stance that comes with blame. If you're like most people, you know this one all too well. WBC can help you remem-ber to take a breath and back off from that defensive, blaming stance when it occurs. Ask yourself before you speak, do I want to win by blaming and proving my point, or do I want to develop a deeper connection and grow closer to him or her? *If you will pause to ask yourself that one question on a regular basis, you will dramatically boost your relationship mojo.*

I always begin relationship counseling sessions by asking the couple if they would like to raise the bar for love and har-mony in their relationship. I declare, "You two are at a choice point," and have them face each other and consider questions like these: "Do you want to be allies? Do you want to work as a team on your issues? Do you want to win and be right, or do you want to be closer to one another and more in love? What is your intention in this session?" In my sessions, as well as in life, being clear about your intentions when communicating with another is first and foremost. Once you realize you are always at a choice point and take the time to get clear about your intentions, then it's time for *straight talk*.

Straight Talk

Whole-body consciousness takes the healthy relating skills mentioned earlier to the next level. Once you learn to witness how an external event (another's words, actions, vocal tone, body language, even a fleeting facial expression) impacts you by utilizing SET, you gain a breadth of awareness that immediately lifts you out of old patterns. Rather than misinterpret, misperceive, or guess what your partner is up to, you simply share your inner experience as the one on the receiving end. That's why I call this "straight talk." It's direct, efficient, and with the use of SET, goes *straight* to the deepest objective truth. It takes practice, but once you develop this skill, you stand on the solid ground of self-responsibility. To return to our example of the little boy waiting in line for the snow cone, you won't be waiting for someone else to tell you that your head itches. Let's start practicing straight talk by telling truth to *ourselves* first.

The following series of questions is designed to help you discover and decipher your particular makeup when it comes to relating to others.

- ⚏ Do you try to control conversations? Sometimes? Often? Never? If you do, are you aware of it in the moment? Do you have conscious reasons for doing this? What are the feelings underlying your effort to control conversations? Nervousness? Impatience? Enthusiasm? Urgency?

:: What feelings come up in you when you meet a new
person? What do you feel when you meet a new person
whom you perceive to be more successful than you? Bigger or smaller than you? Better looking than you? How
comfortable do you feel with others in general? Just reflect
for a moment on any such dynamics in your interactions
with others.

:: Do you tend to hold back in conversations or take a passive role because you lack confidence or don't know how
to fully participate? If you do, are you aware of this in the
moment? Do you have conscious reasons for doing this?
What are the feelings underlying your holding back or
being reserved?

:: Do you "dump" your feelings, opinions, and upsets on
your spouse, family, friends, coworkers, boss? If so, are
you aware of doing this in the moment?

:: Do you withhold your feelings from your spouse, family,
friends, coworkers, or boss? If so, are you aware of doing
this in the moment?

:: Pick three important people in your life. Now, think of
feelings or of anything you would like to share with them
but haven't, for one reason or another. Do you know why
you hold back?

:: Do you habitually cover up your feelings in front of others, whether by being serious, withdrawn, or shut-down;
hyper and chatty; or by making jokes and being flippant?
If so, are you aware of doing what you are doing in the
moment?

:: What percentage of your conversation with others feels
authentic? How often do you share your truth and feel
open to others' truths? How much of your talk to others is
saying what you believe they would like to hear, "selling"

yourself, or trying to make an impression? How aware are you of doing anything like this in the moment?

:: Are you aware of what your body is doing when you talk? Do your hands move? How congruent are you—meaning, do your face and body language match what you're feeling and saying?

Having examined your level of awareness in your relations, do you see patterns you would like to change? Do you have a clear sense of situations where you are generally inhibited, uneasy, or passive—or where you are relatively confident, uninhibited, and dynamic? Do you see sticking points you would like to move beyond? In the next section, you will discover a body-based style of relating that makes this forward motion possible.

Assumptions are the termites of relationships.

—Henry Winkler

Who wants termites chewing at their relationship? Nobody I know, and yet most people I know—myself included——have a head full of useless thoughts that pop up uninvited whenever they move toward another person. The good news is, you can simply witness those thoughts and discard them as readily as the spam that lands in your in-box. One inhale is all it takes to tap WBC and get out of your head and into your body the very next moment. Your body is your number one ally when it comes to communicating successfully.

Ever have the experience that when people say or do a certain thing, you start to edit yourself, shut down, and modify or otherwise change the outward expression of what you feel? Often, we are concerned that others may react negatively to our truth or that they might think poorly of what we say. So we edit or package what we say accordingly.

Your body knows when you are not expressing your full truth for *whatever* reason. As you interact with others, social masks, ill-fitting beliefs, wounds from the past, and a host of other dynamics collaborate to prevent you from embodying your authentic self. When I edit myself to please others or elicit a certain response, I am showing a limited version of myself. I am blocking my authenticity, and by doing so, I ensure and reinforce not being received for who I truly am. My body knows it every time. If I listen to my body, I can catch myself, but when I don't, I feel awkward and uncomfortable. Whether in a business or personal situation, this leads me to anticipate a "no" instead of a "yes." This can be devastating; the consequence is a missed opportunity or a result that is the opposite of my desired outcome. Does this sound familiar to you?

Your body—and the other person's body—knows exactly how truthful you are being in any encounter. That statement bears repeating: *your body—and the other person's body—knows exactly how truthful you are being in any encounter.*

Here's how you can consistently present yourself to the world authentically: tell the truth, the whole truth, and nothing but the truth. Your body will let you know when you begin to edit yourself. Don't ignore it. Presenting your authentic self to the world is ultimately easier than editing your words and behavior to match what you think others want. Use the SET technique to check in and ask your body, "Am I telling the full truth here?" Then take the risk and say, "Take me for who I am; this is the real me." That's when magic happens.

In your quest to be increasingly authentic, dare to explore beneath the surface level of everyday conversation to discover and express whatever you experience without tweaking it. For instance, you may decline a friend's invitation to see a movie together because you don't feel like seeing the movie. On the surface, that's what seems to be true. However, consulting your new ally, your body, you may notice that you are actually fearful in your belly. As you probe deeper, you may realize that you are afraid of how this friend drives; that's the real reason you don't want to go. Now you have an opportunity to tell the whole truth. Obviously, you need to be tactful. But it may very well serve your friend to just say, "I noticed that when you invited me to see the film that I got scared because I don't always feel safe when you're driving." He may choose to be offended, but if he is a real friend, he'll be interested in what you said and maybe even change his driving habits. Either way, tuning in to your deeper truth gives everyone more options.

Another way we obscure meaning in conversation is to unwittingly misuse the words *think, feel, know,* and *believe.* For instance, you might say, "I feel you're making a big mistake," when a friend tells you they are quitting school. You don't actually "feel" someone is making a mistake. It's what your mind "thinks." The word *feel* can only be used to describe a sensation or an emotion *you have.* You feel hungry, angry, happy, etc. In this situation, if you tuned in to your body, you would probably realize you had an emotional reaction to what your friend said. With WBC, you can connect to that feeling and be even more honest. You might say something like, "When you told me about quitting school, I noticed that I felt sad." That's a lot different from "I feel you are making a mistake."

The fact is that no one can *make* you feel anything. Saying "You make me mad" is as inaccurate as saying "You make me weigh 180 pounds." I weigh what I weigh. I feel what I feel. With WBC, we can start to watch our words and experiment with telling it like it is and owning what we feel, think, believe, or know, rather than giving others power over us. It's as simple as SET, asking, "What is the truth right now?" and declaring what is self-evident.

Your relationships with others are always an extension of, and defined by, your relationship with yourself in any moment. Straight talk allows you to find your inner truth in any encounter and act in concert with others in a way that produces the best possible result.

I'm a great believer that any tool that enhances communication has profound effects in terms of how people can learn from each other and how they can achieve the kind of freedoms that they're interested in.

—BILL GATES

One of the key ingredients to straight talk is body-based intimacy. The word *intimacy* comes from the Latin *intimare*, meaning "to press into, to make known." What we "know" can be shared on a verbal level and also a nonverbal somatic level, allowing us to reveal ourselves more deeply.

For instance, Dr. Sharon is a dentist who kept getting into conflict with her office staff. Terrible rifts would arise and make the work environment quite unpleasant not only for her employees but for her patients as well. We got to the root of the problem by employing WBC and taking stock of the unconscious viral beliefs that kept prompting her to scold her staff in a hurtful way. For instance, one day she walked into her office first thing in the morning and saw magazines strewn across the reception area from the previous day. She immediately grabbed the first staff member in sight and berated her. Not a great way to set the tone for the day.

What Dr. Sharon discovered in her WBC session was that whenever anyone hadn't done what she had asked, it triggered a deep seated fear of losing control. In order to establish a sense of control in those situations, she would throw a tantrum, much as she had in her family as a child. When she looked through her adult periscope, she was able to recognize that her office staff was not her family. With WBC, she was able to connect the dots between her behavior and the dynamic she'd grown accustomed to in her family—having her wishes and needs ignored. This recognition alone gave her the space to choose a new approach. The self-fulfilling prophecy of "My needs and desires don't matter" no longer distorted her communication. She began to practice straight talk and was able to embody and emanate a new expectation: that her staff would happily align with her wishes. It worked like magic. Not only was she able to ask for what she really needed, she discovered that she had a knack for inspiring her employees to rally around her vision of a lively office environment that nurtured both clients and staff.

How to Straight-Talk Step-by Step

1. What's so? No spin needed! Just state what's going on matter-of-factly, with no drama, as if you were reporting the time of day: "I walked in and saw magazines sitting on all of the chairs in the reception area."

2. What is my self-evident truth? Again, no spin here. Scan your body, feelings, and emotions, and report the findings: "I notice that my belly feels a little tight and queasy. I feel disappointed, even a little angry."

3. Explain the source of your feelings. And again, no spin. Don't make it about the other party—or, in Dr. Sharon's case, her staff—giving them license to get defensive. This will prevent your getting entangled in a tug-of-war. Simply state your own thoughts: "When I saw the reception area wasn't cleaned up, I had feelings arise about my requests not being honored. I personally have a need, when I arrive for the day, to see that everything is straightened up, and fresh and ready. It helps me set the tone for a fresh day."

4. Ask for what you need. Be sincere. Make sure you are not whining or complaining or sending off threatening body signals: "I am glad I got to tell you how important having the reception area cleaned up in the morning is for me. I appreciate that you listened. I have a request. Before we open for business in the morning, would you be willing to make sure to have the reception area cleaned and ready?"

Dr. Sharon's use of straight talk illustrates how we can use this type of communication in both our personal *and* business lives.

Straight Talk in Business

When I started taking the risk to tell the whole truth in my business dealings, I saw amazing results. I shared the story earlier about telling a purchasing executive my purpose for doing my job, and how refreshed she was to hear it. This gave me an opening to ask her questions about her own business and life. We built a rapport.

Some years later, when my company was taken over, I told the new vice president that I was dissatisfied with his compensation plan and that I noticed I felt less energized about work. He appreciated my being up-front and returned the favor by explaining that the new parent company was eager to clear house, so I had to either accept this compensation plan or quit. In this case, even though I didn't get what I wanted (namely, special treatment as the number one sales representative), I did get something else. From that moment on, the new VP and I trusted each other to tell the truth, even if the resulting information was not what the other wanted to hear. For the rest of my time there, we shared an open dialogue and disregarded corporate politics when it came to our one-on-one communications. We were very different people, but we managed to grow quite close. The lesson here isn't that by telling the truth you will instantly get what you want every time but that sharing your truth creates the possibility for *something* new to happen in the relationship. You can enjoy finding out exactly what that is, and trusting it will be just what is actually needed—if not immediately, then down the road.

I have used the "whole truth" strategy to help management teams develop a new understanding of one another by identifying and sharing their purpose with each other. I've listened with pride and delight to comments like "I never knew the deeper reasons why you worked here, but now I really get it, and I appreciate the role you play." Or, "We've never felt this close in all the years we've worked together. It seems like we're getting to know each other for the first time." And, from a feedback form, "Increasing our BQ has improved communication, morale, and productivity in our office." Straight talk in business helps to break down those artificial barriers we might sum up as "professionalism" and replaces them with a more authentic and effective professional demeanor, informed by whole-body consciousness.

Before you go on to the next chapter, take a big, deep breath. You just finished one of the most exhilarating rides of this adventure.

9

Boost Your Health and Well-Being

The greatest wealth is health.

— Virgil

Health is a state of complete physical, mental, and social well-being, and not merely the absence of disease or infirmity.

—World Health Organization

T HOUGH THE HOLISTIC approach to health may seem like a recent phenomenon, it has been around a long, long time—at least since the days of Hippocrates. Often referred to as "the father of medicine," Hippocrates revolutionized the view of disease by decrying the notion of sickness as punishment from the gods and emphasizing personal responsibility instead. Healing, from his maverick perspective, should take into account lifestyle habits, diet, attitude, environment, and the moral and spiritual condition of a person, which includes one's beliefs.

The challenge most of us face is not whether or not to embrace this perspective; it makes intrinsic sense and cannot be denied if we are interested in personal responsibility. The challenge lies in two specific areas, both of which will be addressed in this chapter: (1) most of us cannot see our own blind spots where our health is concerned and therefore can't seem to get a grip on needed changes in our habits, attitude, environment, etc.; and (2) we lack the specific tools and techniques that are, fortunately, not only easy to use but perpetually available.

First, let's look at one woman's blind spot and how it affected her health. Then, we'll see how WBC helped her lift the veil.

Jennifer was eight years old when her beloved grandfather passed away. Her mother explained his death as best she knew how: "You'll never see Grandpa again, honey. He's in heaven now." Jennifer did not understand why her grandfather was gone, and she felt very angry; her grandpa had always been her favorite babysitter and best friend. *Why did he have to go?* On the day of the funeral, Jennifer was very upset. All those people crying and making a fuss—she just wanted her grandpa back. By the time the service was about to start, Jennifer was fuming mad. Her mother scolded her quietly, insisting that she shouldn't be angry; she should be sad. Jennifer wanted to scream. She didn't dare aggravate her mother any further, so she held her breath to keep from yelling out her confusion and pain. The scream built up in her chest until she felt as if a sharp blade had pierced her sternum. A few days later, she began to have difficulty breathing. Her mother took her to the pediatrician. The doctor's diagnosis: asthma.

It was during one of my seminars that Jennifer's story came out. I had asked the participants to express their greatest desire, and Jennifer shared that hers was simply to be able to take full, deep breaths. She'd been to numerous clinics and specialists over the years, but nothing had helped relieve her asthma. I had her do the self-evident truth exercise at the front of the room. After attempting to take a full breath, she reported that her chest and lungs hurt. Her throat felt constricted, and even speaking became difficult. With my encouragement, she continued to take deep breaths, and when I asked her to say out loud what she desired, she declared, "I want to breathe easier and feel healthy—strong and capable." After repeating her desire several times, she noticed the feelings in her chest and throat intensify. She followed the sensations, keenly aware of her whole body, breathing rhythmically for several minutes until the sensations in her chest and throat led her right to their origin. In her mind's eye, she was back in the vestibule of the church where her mother had scolded her. Her hand came up to her chest as the pain there intensified. "Oh my God," she said, "That's when I started having trouble breathing!"

Until that moment, she had no idea that the feelings she had repressed about her grandfather's passing could be linked to her asthma. I asked her to breathe and repeat after me, "I want to take big, full breaths and be healthier, *and* I am afraid to feel the pain and express my anger about my grandfather's death." Jennifer repeated the words several times and began rocking her body back and forth until suddenly a spine-chilling scream came out of her mouth, shaking the room and all of us in it. The anger and pain that had been kept down for thirty years blasted out of Jennifer's mouth like a blowtorch. I encouraged Jennifer to thank her lungs for storing all that frustration and rage for so long and to tell them they were now relieved of duty. She took a full, deep breath and said, "My lungs, my lungs—I can breathe!"

Get It Off Your Chest

You've probably heard stories like Jennifer's, in which someone achieves physical relief by finally speaking out and releasing what has been repressed. Just think about how many times you've heard someone say, "I am so happy that I finally told my boss about such and such. . . . I'd been holding onto that for months. It feels so good to get it off of my chest." Ever take the risk to tell it like it is and immediately feel the heaviness on your chest lift? Or, like Jennifer, finally clear an emotional dam that may have been holding back the river of your emotions for years?

As I've said many times throughout this book, your body-mind is a remarkable organism that records and stores every detail of your existence. As a *system*, your body-mind seeks homeostasis; it will improvise and adapt to keep on functioning—even if that functioning is subpar. Underlying any and all such adaptations is a fundamental urge or drive toward well-being. This is what we tap into when we access whole-body consciousness in the context of establishing optimal health.

Let's look closely at Jennifer's scenario, which I described earlier. Here we have a little girl whose body-mind is confronted with a combination of stressors that coincide in space and time. First comes the stress of being told that she will never see her beloved grandparent again. Then, on top of that shock comes the stress of seeing a whole bunch of adults in tears—adults whom Jennifer ordinarily sees as quite capable and on top of things. This spells mounting tension and confusion for an eight-year-old. Jennifer has no brothers, sisters, or cousins to soften the blow with their companionship; she is facing the situation without peer support or even a yardstick to measure her own reaction. Then family members begin to convene at the church. Jennifer is angry that her grandfather is not there to hold her hand as he usually does at family gatherings. A long, black station wagon pulls up in front of the church. When the casket is rolled out and her father and uncles flank the shiny box covered with flowers, it hits her· *My grandpa is in there!* Jennifer's inner Richter scale registers 8.2—a major quake. And moments later comes a big aftershock—her mother's bugaboo: *Don't feel what you feel.* The message is clear: *It's not appropriate to be mad; that's not allowed. Stop it now.* Jennifer wants to scream, but her body-mind cannot take one more stressor, cannot risk her mother's rejection should she fail to obey. So her body-mind adapts and does the best it can and puts a lid on the scream. A heavy lid—like a steel manhole cover. All of this happens in an instant, subconsciously. The adaptation is in place. The seed has just been planted. Days later, it sends up a shoot, and Jennifer is unable to simply *breathe*.

Get Your Life Force Out of Storage

It is a widely acknowledged fact that stress and tension can induce body-mind disorders that lead to chronic health problems. Jennifer's natural feelings of anger were unable to run their course; this placed undue stress on her young body. Said another way, holding all that tension in put her system on overload and thus disturbed her life force.

Our bodies are not designed to be storage sheds. When you fill up with emotion, you need a reliable way to clear it out to avoid becoming overloaded with stress. Research shows that 80 to 90 percent of all doctor visits are stress related. Many illnesses originate from holding in feelings and overloading the system with stress. You can use whole-body consciousness to check in with your body and empty your tank of stress whenever you notice the pressure building inside. WBC can also alleviate many aches and pains that are caused by unconsciously tensing certain areas in your body. Using the SET technique is a bit like restarting your computer; increased clarity and vitality is the natural result.

When we take responsibility for listening to these bodies that we live in, we take our health in our own hands. When we empty ourselves of toxic thoughts and beliefs and explore emotions that have been repressed and stored in the subconscious, the body's natural restorative power takes over.

Listen to the Voice of the Body

The patient should be made to understand that he or she must take charge of his own life. Don't take your body to the doctor as if he were a repair shop.

—QUENTIN REGESTEIN, M.D., associate professor
of psychiatry, Harvard Medical School

The quote above refers to one of the most important forks in the road we all come to at some point in life. It's that moment when we stop relying solely on external authority and lean into our inner authority by taking personal responsibility for our health. This doesn't mean we don't go to doctors or heed their advice—it means we work with them to discover what the body-mind needs to function at its best. Author and men's movement leader Sam Keen describes the process this way: "The path from illness to health seems to move through three stages: the experience of the body as victim of illness, listening to the voice of the body, and accepting responsibility for creating disease and healing the body-mind and spirit."

This reminds me of my client Barry, who arrived one day for a session complaining of flu symptoms. Applying Keen's three-stage model, Barry was in the first stage: he said that his body was under attack by a virus. He reported pain in his belly and was alternating between feeling feverish and feeling chilled. His mind was spinning with worries: *Will I miss work? How long will I be sick?* These thoughts caused him to tense up and feel even worse. His muscles were tight, and he ached all over. When we assume the victim position, we tend to create downward thoughts to help us avoid facing whatever our body is feeling in the moment. I asked Barry, "Would you be willing to use the WBC tools to discover what this illness is telling you?" He nodded yes.

First, I encouraged him to disengage from his spin thoughts using the SET technique. He tapped into his self-evident truth and stated out loud that his stomach muscles were tight and that this particular stomach pain was very familiar. I asked him to explore what emotions might be linked to this pain. He said, "Fear. I feel unsafe, unsure, and helpless." After repeating this several times, his body started contracting, as if he was trying to hide. I asked Barry if hiding was a familiar feeling, and he said, "Yes. This is exactly like the pain I felt many times when my stepdad was beating my mom. I would hide behind the sofa with my brother; we were both terrified that he would beat us up too. I felt so sad and powerless watching my mom getting hurt. I remember now how I held my tummy in, stopped breathing, and crumpled up like a piece of paper, tight, in fear, worried about what might happen next. Through the years I tried to act as if it didn't happen or wasn't affecting me, but I can see now that this has lived inside me all these years."

I invited him to say and do whatever his body was unable to do back then. Barry slowly moved out of the contracted position, sat up, and said, "Stop hurting my mom!" He swung his arms and pounded the floor, saying the words over and over with increasing strength. I encouraged him to vent fully and to make his movements bigger. After several minutes, Barry's eyes opened wide; they had been half-shut all day. He reported that all of his body pain had vanished, and he felt immensely relieved.

Half the problem with symptoms that resemble the onset of a flu or cold lies in our reaction to discomfort. We worry and spin like crazy, causing the body to tighten up and constrict, which blocks the natural healing response that comes through relaxation. The next time you feel ill or experience pain, get out of your head and embrace the discomfort. See if you can trace your feelings back to their source and express what your body wants to express instead of contracting and adding more stress to the system.

Another client, Andy, learned a big lesson about how putting feelings away can cause one pain later on. Andy had suffered from back pain every day for eight years. With whole-body consciousness, he embraced his pain and explored it to discover its source. He'd been avoiding the tax man for years. The thought of paying his back taxes made him so uncomfortable that he continued to avoid the IRS, despite his better judgment. Almost daily, he would tell himself, "Just shove the problem to the back of your mind." Ironically, Andy was a chiropractor who held the belief that our thoughts and words go directly to our medulla oblongata—the hindmost part of the brain that exits the skull and enters into our spine. So when Andy put his words and thoughts in the back of his mind, he literally put them in *the back of his mind*, and they flowed through his skull and into his spine, creating pain. Every choice we make has both a cost and a potential payoff. Andy's payoff was to "forget" about the IRS and go another day without paying; his cost was chronic back pain. Once he contacted the IRS and cleared his tax debt, his pain disappeared. It has not returned since.

Don't take your problems out on your body! The more you explore what is happening in your body and engage in mind-body conversations, the more you can align with what your body needs to simply feel good. If you ignore or abuse your body, it may get sick just to get your attention. Listening to your body puts your feet firmly on the road to better health.

Weight Management: The Cardinal Rule Is for the Birds

Eating habits are formed early in life, and many of us were taught to view food as something other than fuel. For many of us, food equals love. In America, food has become both cheap entertainment and a favorite high-priced pastime. A study in the *Journal of the American Dietetic Association* suggests that parents stop teaching their children the once-popular cardinal rule of the dinner table, "clean your plate, eat it all." According to the professional dieticians who conducted this particular study, this type of training contributes to overeating and obesity. The study showed that when three-year-olds were served bigger than usual portions of macaroni and cheese, they ate what they wanted and stopped when they were full. But the same experiment, done a couple years later, showed that the five-year-olds had already learned to ignore the *body signals* that told them when they'd had enough to eat and instead ate more whenever they were served more.

Using WBC, you can change old beliefs, such as "gotta clean my plate," that no longer serve your health and well-being. Here's how it works. Let's say you are concerned about your excess weight and have decided to stop thinking in circles about it and talk to your body instead. Say aloud, "I want to lose *X* number of pounds." Notice how you feel having said this. Use the SET technique to explore what is occurring in your body and express it. For example, "I notice that when I said I want to lose thirty pounds, my jaw tightened and I felt afraid, as if my one joy—food—would be taken away." Keep breathing. Move your body and express any other feelings.

Now think back to a time, if there ever was one, when you were OK with how your body looked. Notice how the memory feels in your body now. If you never loved your body, acknowledge that and notice how that feels. Likewise, if you love your body now more than ever, feel how that feels. Next, pay particular attention to the areas of your body you want to improve. Say aloud, "I release you from holding any unexpressed feelings. I thank you and free you from being a holding tank for my feelings. I want a new relationship with you, in which you can function at your best." Use these words or create your own body dialogue. And then listen to your body talking back.

Do this once or twice a day—just before eating, for best results. Witness how you interact with your body. Becoming more aware of your BQ is essential to healthy weight management. Start conversing with your body in this way, and you will have higher body-esteem as well as a happier, healthier body.

Exercise and a healthy diet are, of course, of utmost importance; I recommend both highly. WBC can vastly improve any exercise routine, whether you work out at the gym, jog, play tennis, ride a bike, or engage in any other form of exercise. WBC tools can help you move through mental or physical blocks. Next time you feel or think, *I can't do one more rep, or run another step, or serve one more ace,* just pause and practice the SET technique. It may be that you really have reached

your limit, but it may also be that your mind is v
ping you. SET can put you in touch with what is re.
on so that you can expand beyond self-imposed, a
limits. Once you are proficient at WBC techniques, y. can
catch downward and wayward thoughts and reverse them by
breathing and choosing to think upward thoughts. A simple
mind-body intervention such as this can carry you over you
the finish line. In many sports, technique is key; WBC is an
instant tuning fork for any technique that involves BQ. One
breath, and you are back in proper form, performing at your
best.

The more you raise your BQ, the more you will love your
body. When you consciously love and connect with your
body, all movement and exercise becomes more integrated
and enjoyable. A higher BQ equals higher performance, more
vitality, and more fun.

Your Achilles Heel Can Be Your Strength

If at first the idea is not absurd, then there is no hope for it.
— ALBERT EINSTEIN

Long-standing health problems are reversed. Cancerous conditions go into complete remission. Lifelong psychological
issues instantaneously resolve. Ulcers and fibroids and hem-
orrhoids—even a few hernias—have been known to vanish
overnight. Seemingly miraculous, sudden cures such as these
happen with startling regularity. For those who are sick or otherwise afflicted, anecdotal evidence—hundreds if not thousands of stories like Jennifer's—abounds. For some, it induces
only an eye roll; for others, it's enough to inspire a renewal
of faith. But physical healing brought about by nonphysical

means is no longer the exclusive province of faith healers and metaphysicians.

Mind–body medicine is at the forefront of scientific investigation. Dr. Norman Shealy, author of *Soul Medicine*, calls the implications of such research "stunning." Shealy says, "By changing our consciousness, we can change the very blueprints around which our physical bodies are constructed. We can first seek healing close to the source by intervening in our own thinking rather than trying to deal—much later down the line—with the ill effects of our thoughts on our bodies. While it is unlikely that we will ever be able to bypass physical means like drugs and surgery for the healing of every disease in every person, these new insights show clearly that soul medicine is the very first intervention point we should look to for physical or emotional healing."

Early in the twentieth century, Walter Cannon made a breakthrough discovery when he identified the relationship between external events and an acute neuroendocrine response in animals. This led him to coin the familiar phrase *fight-or-flight response*. Cannon was studying primitive reflexes that activate the central nervous system as well as the adrenal glands when perceived danger or environmental pressures present a threat to an animal's life.

A contemporary of Cannon, Dr. Hans Selye, also studied the impact that threatening external events have on an organism. Prior to Selye's work, we had no word for stress; he coined the term and posited the first theories on stress while working on what, in those days, was known as "general adaptation syndrome."

For our purposes, it is important to note the two main components of the physiology of stress: (1) adaptive responses, which include faster pulse rate, increased respiration, muscle tension, and glandular function, and (2) the pathology that

develops when stress is ongoing without relief. Eve[
with a very high BQ face quite a challenge when .. ..
to the first component; it is difficult to interrupt adaptive
responses, especially since many of them occur automatically.
However, you can avoid the buildup of stress and gain relief.
This is where WBC helps you hit the ground running rather
than turning into roadkill when faced with a stressful situation. Once you get accustomed to using the SET technique,
you can do it anytime, anywhere. This simple practice allows
you to reset your nervous system, to "clear the hard drive," so
to speak, of unnecessary residue.

Awareness + *technique* + *sustained application* = *self-mastery*

Following this simple equation, you can turn any weakness
around so that it becomes your strength.

SOS: Your Instant Stress Reduction Tool

The myriad ways in which stress impacts the human body
are determined in part by the sensitivity of the sympathetic
nervous system (SNS). Crucial to our understanding of the
effects of stress is a recognition that the human body mind did
not evolve under constant unrelenting threat. Fight-or-flight
responses were reserved for true emergencies. Those of us with
especially stressful lives are crisis-driven; we live in ready-for-
anything mode and rarely get a break from that constant tension. Even on our days off, we carry around a mobile phone or
e-mail device. The accumulated energy of being on alert all
the time needs to be discharged. Without an outlet, the body
cannot find its way to a state of balance. Once you activate
whole-body consciousness, you become attuned to your own
body and can make the choice to come back to center as soon
as you recognize downward or wayward thoughts.

Study after study has shown that stress has a negative impact on the functioning of the immune system, thus making us even more susceptible to disease. It seems certain that stress is a major contributing factor in the disease process. Long before disease manifests, however, many of us are operating in what Dr. Henry Han, O.M.D., calls "the grey zone"—that subpar state of being that makes "do your best" sound a bit like "go move a mountain." Han, the coauthor of *Ancient Herbs, Modern Medicine*, defines this in-between state as "a ubiquitous yet generally overlooked area between the state of health and the state of disease . . . in essence, a state of imbalance."

For example, let's say you have recurrent anxiety symptoms. Even minor emotional upsets get you riled, and major ones are ever-present given your lifestyle and the era in which you live. You're feeling emotionally burned out and on the verge of exhaustion. You can't change your lifestyle overnight, and yet you're almost out of energy reserves. If you stay in this downward spiral, you will collapse in complete exhaustion. You can see the writing on the walls.

WBC changes all that; in fact, it actually *increases* your energy level. This is because WBC provides a direct doorway to your parasympathetic nervous system (PNS). The PNS is the complement to the sympathetic nervous system. Said simply, it's the "rest and digest" mode that follows "fight or flight." Consider what family practitioner Maureen Traub, M.D., reported about using the SET technique with patients in her office:

> When clients come to my office to be diagnosed, they are often anxious, and their sympathetic nervous systems are operating. This results in dilated pupils, tight muscles, and pounding hearts. After a few minutes of doing the self-evident truth exercise, they relax, and

their parasympathetic nervous system clicks in, allowing them to tune in to what they are feeling in their body cognitively. That helps me diagnose better and them heal faster. When I use the SET as part of my healing modality, patients become more receptive to whatever I prescribe. The results have been phenomenal.

Applying the SET technique activates the parasympathetic nervous system and calms the fight-or-flight response. Here's how it works: Pause and close your eyes the minute you feel a crisis brewing, get some disappointing news, or are knocked off balance by a shocking event. Take a deep breath and, if you can, look around to find a safe place to sit down. Feel your feet on the ground. Now scan your body and let go of any obvious tension, or simply notice the tension if you cannot let it go. Breathe in and out very slowly, drawing the breath in through your nostrils rather than through your open mouth. Your mind may still be racing; that's to be expected.

Now, here's the key—continue breathing very slowly in and out of your nose, and when a troublesome thought comes into your mind, open your mouth and start blowing in and out rapidly for several moments. Then return to slow nostril breathing. Continue these last two steps until you feel at ease. Trust me, if you can just give yourself that one-minute break, you will be very pleased at the results.

Sound health can be yours when you claim it and do the inner work that clears a path for healing to occur. In the words of Louise Hay, from *Heal Your Body*, "The word *incurable*, which is so frightening to so many people, really only means that the particular condition cannot be cured by outer methods and that we must go within to effect the healing. The condition came from nothing and will go back to nothing."

CHAPTER

10

Boost Your Prosperity

*I know of no more encouraging fact than the unquestionable
ability of man to elevate his life by a conscious endeavor.*

—Henry David Thoreau, *Walden*

*You have brains in your head. You have feet in your shoes.
You can steer yourself any direction you choose.*

Dr. Seuss, *Oh, the Places You'll Go!*

I HAD PUT THE better part of six years into building rock-solid relationships with customers, coworkers, and support staff. My corporate job was more or less on autopilot and extremely lucrative. Then, one day, my body simply said, "Enough!" and dug in its heels, refusing to return to the office for any purpose other than to clean out my desk and say a few good-byes. I had completely lost my drive to sell even one more piece of business equipment. I called my regional manager first and told him how I was feeling. Then I phoned my family and closest friends. Everyone I spoke with that morning essentially said the same thing: "You know what you feel and you have to follow that . . . *but* . . . you have your gig so wired . . . loyal customers . . . and a six-figure income . . . why quit?"

Proactive by Design

Conflicted, and not wanting to be reckless, I decided to take some time off and allow whole-body consciousness to show me what to do. So I flew to San Diego to spend a few days at Murrieta Hot Springs, known affectionately to the locals as "Club Mud."

After three days of enjoying the quiet, practicing whole-body consciousness, and slathering my body with rich clay, I got it. The time had come to shift my focus. Rather than putting 80 percent of my energy into my job and 20 percent into music, writing, and teaching, I would apply myself 100 percent to what I loved most. When I made that decision, my entire body relaxed. I ran back to my room, closed my eyes, and turned on my tape recorder. I continued breathing deeply and asked, *What I should do?* As I asked the question, an image appeared in my mind's eye. I saw a large group of people; I was standing in the middle of the crowd. I stayed with the vision, and the "what" that my inner knowing was revealing became more and more clear. Marin County professionals had few places to meet and network outside of chamber of commerce meetings. The time had come for me to address this need and start a networking group. I spoke my intention into the tape recorder: "I will do two things when I get home. First, I will resign. Second, I will find a location willing to host the first ever 'Marin Business Exchange.'"

Upon my return to Marin, I approached the manager of a popular restaurant in Sausalito and promised that if he would offer free hors d'oeuvres, I would fill his bar with people the following Monday night. Deal, he said. I placed a single ad in the local newspaper, and 240 eager networkers showed up. As they walked through the door, I introduced myself to each person, saying, "Hi! I'm Steve Sisgold, your host. I can help you create your dreams." By the time the last stuffed mushroom had been consumed, I had eight new clients. I have never looked back.

The Marin Business Exchange grew and thrived over the next three years. To this very day, I run into folks who tell me stories of the great connections—friendships, business partnerships, even a marriage or two—that grew out of those meetings. Not once have I regretted the decision to let go of the certainty of employment and a regular paycheck. My mind-body approach to helping people grow their business and live their dreams spread quickly. Within a few short months, I began to coach authors, recording artists, business executives, and medical professionals. Clients came to my home office for hours, weekends, and even weeks at a time, while we cleared the debris inside and designed action plans. I was awarded a gold record for my contribution to a Grammy Award–winning artist whose album stayed on the top of the *Billboard* charts for over twenty weeks. The work—and the achievements people experienced having discovered WBC—caught on like wildfire. In order to accommodate all of the requests I was getting for consultations, I started a series of "success support groups." I had three groups of twenty people each meeting at my home office in Marin, and other long-term groups that met over a period of years. I had the pleasure of coleading one of these groups with bestselling author Gay Hendricks.

One WBC success support group member, a thirty-six-year-old sales representative named Harold, could sell his product easily to men. Around female buyers, however, he became anxious and frequently blew the sale. At one of our group sessions, Harold tapped into WBC and got to the root of the problem. As a boy, he had often felt overwhelmed by his domineering mother and found it difficult to express himself around her. His tongue seemed to go brain-dead as he stumbled with his words, and he'd eventually shut down. Feeling where this memory lived in his body–mind allowed Harold to recognize his triggers and get a grip on how he managed himself when working with a woman in a position of authority. With the help of WBC exercises, he was able to rewire himself so that he could relax with female buyers. This doubled his potential customer base; his sales volume quickly followed suit. And, most important, he cleared the rather large roadblock that had resided in his body for so many years.

Another group member wondered why she couldn't create a successful business as a clothing designer. Gabrielle had a knack for design. The dresses she dreamed up and sewed together were a mix of classic lines and special feminine flair. But she resisted taking her designs out to the world. I had her say what she wanted aloud to the group. She said, "I want to be a successful clothing designer and seamstress." When I had her say this again and invited her to practice SET, she noticed her bodily reactions and reported them to the group: "I feel sad and small." This simple declaration led Gabrielle to recognize the link between her desire and her father's disapproval. Next I had her express her "desire" and her "but . . ." as we did in Chapter 5.

Turning Negative Equations into Success Formulas

I'll break down Gabrielle's experience of the exercise as a way to review the basic principle.

> "I want to be a successful artist, (desire)
> but
> my father will disapprove." (viral belief)

I then asked her, "What does your father's disapproval represent to you? And how does that make you feel?" She said,

"I'll be rejected, and that makes me feel afraid." Gabrielle identified the primary viral belief that stood between her and a successful career. She had also taken the first step toward changing that belief in her body-mind.

Next I had her look at what fed this viral belief and led her to construct the negative equation. Through WBC, she recalled that when she was a young woman, her dad would leave the room in disgust whenever she voiced her desire to become a professional clothing designer. She felt rejected and afraid; those reactions had been simmering in her unconscious for years. Gabrielle's negative equation looked like this:

Being creative, a designer = father's disapproval
Father's disapproval = abandonment
Abandonment = fear and rejection

To change her formula, I helped Gabrielle rework the equation into something positive that would give her confidence and help her create success.

Being creative = approval
Approval = closeness
Closeness = nurturing love

Gabrielle didn't wait for her father to change his mind; she changed her own. From that place, his judgment ceased to influence her decisions. She began to embody her creativity and her desire more and more. Today, she is sole proprietor of a flourishing clothing design firm. For Father's Day, she was able to buy her dad a set of golf clubs he had been wishing for. She was both surprised and pleased to hear him admit, "I guess I had you all wrong."

Now it's your turn to change your negative equations into powerful success formulas.

1. State something you want. Say it out loud or silently and notice your bodily reactions. Now take several deep breaths. Give your body full permission to do whatever it wants. Feel your feelings and identify any inner blocks that stand in the way of that desire blossoming into a reality.

I want _____
_____.

Now, add what's blocking you.

I want _____
_____,

but _____
_____.

Notice how you feel.

2. Now, create your own equation from the viral belief and feelings you have just uncovered.

_____ (desire) = _____ (viral belief)

_____ (viral belief) = _____ (negative result)

_____ (negative result) = _____ (uncomfortable feelings)

3. Now create your positive, productive equation with a positive outcome and good feelings.

_____ (desire) = _____ (healthy belief)

_____ (healthy belief) = _____ (positive result)

_____ (positive result) = _____ (comfortable feelings)

For both Harold and Gabrielle, external circumstances were not the cause of their repeatedly putting the brakes on success. It wasn't the economy, the marketplace, or another person. For Gabrielle, it was a body-based fear of rejection, and for Harold, a fear of being overwhelmed or controlled. Using WBC to change their negative equations into empowering ones led to a breakthrough; it can do the same for you.

Failure exists primarily in your perception. If you could see the big picture from where you stand, you would know defeat as a catalyst, an invitation to grow. The spark of new inspiration is only a breath away.

With the help of WBC, when a challenging or difficult situation arises, you can count on your body to show you the way through rather than collapsing, withdrawing, or getting caught in a spin trap. When you get out of your head and use WBC, you take charge of your career, your finances, and your overall direction in life. Below are proven systems, success formulas, and key questions that will help you fully embody what you truly desire. Essential areas of your life will naturally and easily rearrange around this new, more authentic, and more intentional you.

Be the CEO of Your Life

Once you rewire your thinking and embody a positive equation, it's time to create a success plan, integrate and implement new strategies, and begin to take action.

Working in the corporate world taught me that structure has its benefits. When I left my job, I decided to apply the company flowchart model to my life. So I appointed myself the CEO of Sisgold, Unlimited. I reasoned that the CEO of a corporation should know better than to neglect a single product division in his company, because profitability depends on his attention to the entire company. Is it really much different in this business called life? With no overarching vision and flow-chart, I was prone to making impulsive decisions and ignoring some very important aspects of my life. Like most people, I reacted by default instead of being proactive by design. This common behavior is problematic for a number of reasons. First, it makes for messes that then require time and energy to clean up. And second, it can lead you to unnecessary dead ends if you follow impulses that leave your true priorities in the lurch.

So I sat down one afternoon and worked up an executive summary of sorts. First I examined my life and looked at the key divisions or areas that were crucial to the success of Sisgold, Unlimited. Then, using WBC principles and processes, I generated a detailed plan for each area. The "CEO action plan" below will take you step-by-step through this very same process. You may very well have done exercises like this in the past, and yet I know that using SET to test how you feel about each piece of the plan will give the process greater depth and dimension. You can also use SET to "beat the bushes" on your fears and chase them out into the open where the viral beliefs that feed them can be challenged.

Think of your family and friends, as well as your creator or any other positive force, as possible stockholders in your company. These people depend on you as the CEO to be accountable for every action and its results. Keep them in mind when you consider your commitments, and make a conscious choice about what you can give yourself over to and get behind 100 percent. Also give some thought to what individuals you will invite to sit on the board of directors of You, Unlimited.

The divisions include all the areas of your life that are most important to you: health, career, relationships, relaxation, fun, personal growth, and so forth. Each division also has subsidiaries.

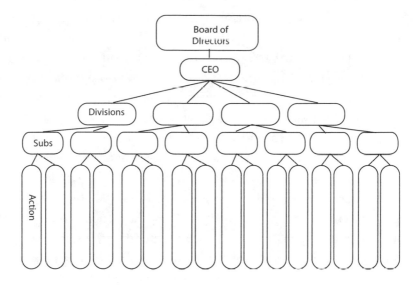

Having your priorities and desires clearly mapped out in this way greatly assists you in staying on track and moving in the direction of what you really want. It is the process of making the chart that helps you really establish your priorities. So please take extra care in crafting it. Establishing priorities and desires helps you stay organized and on time. Of course, keeping your word is essential too. All of these elements together give you a rock-solid foundation upon which to create the life of your dreams.

Instead of being forced into action by default, you follow your plan. Practice the SET technique as you make decisions throughout the day; speak your options aloud at choice points and notice how your body responds. Only make choices that register in your body as truly aligned with your purpose. If your body says "no," work with the SET process to clarify what it is you need and can act on with confidence in that circumstance. With practice, WBC becomes a reliable barometer that can show you whether a belief is holding you back or whether the choice you are about to make is simply not right for you.

Listen to all of the minds in your body as you prepare your CEO chart. This will build your connection with your inner-most self, where true knowledge resides. Most of us have histori-cally had little more than a dial-up connection with our insides. If you have made it this far in this book and have worked with the practices, it's likely you now have the equivalent of a high-speed connection. This analogy may seem a bit far-fetched to you; it doesn't to me. I once knew a man whose habit of call-ing a psychic any time he was faced with a difficult decision became quite expensive. He spent more per month on psychics than the average resident of San Francisco spends on parking tickets. Eventually, as was inevitable, this client had become overly dependent on that connection with an outer authority. His inner authority and ability to trust what he knew inside himself was difficult for him to access. I believe in working with coaches, counselors, therapists, you name it, but I rely on my inner knowing first—and last. The more we lean on an exter-nal structure, the less opportunity our internal structure gets to grow strong through bearing the weight of decision. These practices and the intentional focus they foster will encourage that development. So let's consider the three minds in the body so that you can call on them as you work on your CEO chart.

I find it useful to pay special attention to these distinctions: the brain-mind, the heart-mind, and the gut-mind. The brain-mind's job is to come up with clear, well-thought-out answers. Its weakness, as we have seen, is a tendency to make ego-based decisions that don't serve you, because they stem from viral beliefs or an unresolved event in the past. The heart-mind's strength is compassion and love, although the heart can also turn on you with strong emotions like jealousy that lead to wildly off-balance decisions. Residual wounds and feelings from earlier, similar heartbreaks and betrayals can fog your thinking and feeling. The gut-mind makes its decisions based on that "yes" or "no" that is largely nonverbal and comes from deep in your belly. The weakness of the gut-mind lies in its susceptibility to survival-based fears that cloud the decision-making process or preempt it, as the case may be. What we know about the brain is that certain threats register far too quickly for cognition to intervene. You feel these hardwired protective reflexes when you are exposed to heights or snakes. (These two fears are known to exist in all humans across all cultures.)

When all three brains give you a green light on a decision or direction, you will feel the voice of your spirit confirm with a big *Yes.* I feel warm all over when this happens and anticipate that some unforeseen benefit is in store. Generally, a few challenges are also in store, and yet your spirit is unafraid. Your spirit has quite an advanced radar system and can seek out which precise challenge will bring about the most growth. So enjoy making wholehearted decisions, following your gut feelings, and having a clear mind as you set up your CEO action plan. Refuse to ignore anything your body tells you. Something as simple as an ache in your foot can be warning you to reconsider a decision.

Now it's time for you to sketch out your own CEO action plan. Here are some questions to guide you. As you answer each one, practice the SET technique and speak aloud anything you notice that your body is telling you.

:: **Professional.** What are your professional and business goals?
:: **Financial.** What are your goals with respect to income, investment, and savings?
:: **Educational.** What knowledge, expertise, or skills do you want to acquire?
:: **Networking.** What new professional contacts do you want to develop?

:: **Organizations.** What organizations do you want to join and become actively involved in?

:: **Image.** What kind of image do you want to project?

:: **Family.** What kind of relationship do you want with your spouse, your children, your extended family, and your friends?

:: **Home.** What type of environment do you want to live in?

:: **Hobbies.** What interests do you want to actively pursue?

:: **Health/recreation/exercise.** How will you keep yourself healthy, fit, relaxed, and calm?

:: **Personal Growth.** In what areas do you need to develop yourself on a personal and spiritual level?

:: **Fun.** How will you create fun and laughter in your life?

Below is my chart to use as an example.

Now (or later on) go back to page 183 and fill out your CEO chart. You can also transfer the chart to the color poster of your choice to hang in your office or home.

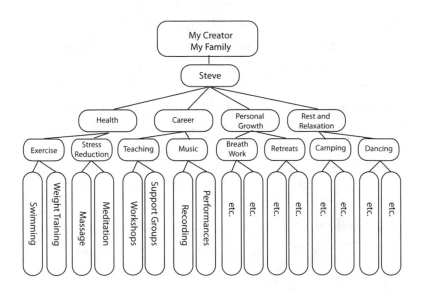

Taking Personal Time

It is important to schedule time to rest, create, visualize, and meditate. We all need time off to rejuvenate, quiet the system, and simply listen. This is the intention behind the tradition of many religions that call for a day of rest, setting time aside to go within and let go of worldly activities. Many cultural traditions have evolved some pattern to formalize "down time." You can take a day or decide to take a fifteen-minute siesta every afternoon. What's important is that you take some time alone to contemplate. Learning to stop *doing* and simply *be* is essential. Don't assume you will get bored, or accept the tired excuse, *I'm too busy.* Carve time out of a day to drop in and drink at the well of nourishment that comes when you sit quietly and absorb into the silence of being. Many of us avoid this practice out of a subliminal fear of being alone and facing the feelings we usually avoid by staying busy. Put your version of a Sabbath rest in your CEO plan.

Power Spots

Set up a sanctuary space in your home to remind you of the importance of your inner life. I visit my walk-in bedroom closet a couple of times each day, and not just to get a new shirt. I have a number of personal symbols on the wall in my closet along with a copy of my purpose statement, a few key affirmations, a list of my strengths and values, and my CEO chart. I read these reminders every day. I take a breath and feel grateful to live another day. You can set up your own power spots in your home, office, and even in your car. Set up a corner for meditation and be very deliberate about what you place there, knowing that the objects are meant to remind you of the path you are on. The body-mind can train toward success in this way. Power spots help you to keep the fire alive and your heart's desires front and center. For example, not until I set up a music room in my house did I begin seriously rehearsing songs I had written to record. My CDs needed an inspiring place to be born; they are now alive and well and neatly packaged.

Also important to remember is the fact that our bodies *love* organization. Cluttered space makes for a cluttered mind. Whereas uncluttered space makes for an uncluttered mind and, as we have seen, an uncluttered body. When my home or office is in disarray, my mind and my body feel the same way. I advise all of my clients to free their lives of unnecessary clutter, even if it means hiring an organizer or feng shui expert for help. Clients often report that taking just this step frees up tremendous creative energy.

In order for your CEO chart/plan to come to life and create the success you desire, you need to get your entire body and being behind your goals and make a strong commitment from head to toe. The dictionary points out that one connotation of the word *commitment* is "entanglement or struggle," but that is not a complete definition. The exercises in this book have likely helped you get in touch with some of the conflicts in your own body, the limiting beliefs, and the sabotaging behaviors. Clearing those gives you the solid foundation you need to make commitments that your body and mind agree with 100 percent—without conflict, entanglement, or struggle. The beauty of a truly aligned commitment is the certainty and relaxation that it brings you, freeing you up to feel joyful. And once you are living your joy, new possibilities and opportunities arise naturally.

Let's explore your commitment status with a few questions. Remember, the mind can trick you into thinking something, but the body never lies.

1. If you had no limits and there was nothing in your way, what would you like to see change in your life? Answer this question to yourself or out loud and listen to your body response:

I want _____

_____.

2. How committed are you to having what you just said you want? What did your body tell you? Tune in to your body and listen to its answer: _____ percent.

3. Now combine saying your desire with how committed you are to having that: I am _____ percent committed to (getting what you just said you want) _____

_____.

4. Practice SET. How does it feel to be _____ percent committed? _____

_____.

5. Declare the truth about that. For instance, "I notice my face tighten, and I am sad that I am only 50 percent committed to making my business fly." _____

_____.

If you are 50 percent committed to a project or your finances, you'll get 50 percent results. If that is what you consciously choose and know it's the truth, then you may find peace with that self-awareness. However, a focused plan backed up with your 100 percent commitment—mind, body, and heart—will increase your results and keep a vital flow of passion ever present in your life. Think about other changes that you would like to see happen in your life, and ask yourself how committed you are to achieving those changes. Listen to what your *body* has to say.

Visioning

Increasing awareness is always the key to initiating change, so let's continue visioning your life. Enjoy filling out your visioning chart on the next page and remember the words of the wise Dr. Seuss that you read at the beginning of this chapter while doing so.

Now that you have your CEO plan, you are ready to begin manifesting each step with wild enthusiasm, perhaps even reckless abandon! In the next chapter, I will share a number of daily rituals that will help you maintain a high level of whole-body consciousness. Day to day, you will discover that your body is your greatest ally, and relying on it for guidance will help you follow through on the intentions you clarified and committed to in your CEO plan.

≡ Visioning Chart ≡

I ENVISION AND DESIRE BY (DATE)	BUSINESS VISION(S)	RELATIONSHIPS VISION(S)	HEALTH VISION(S)	PERSONAL GROWTH VISION(S)
My present situation concerning these visions is (where it stands now):				
How I feel about where they are now:				
I am moved toward my vision by (purpose, joy, money, self-expression):				
I am _____ percent committed to take the following actions to improve my life (today through _____ date):				

CHAPTER

≡ 11 ≡

Practice Makes Perfect

You will never change your life until you change something you do daily.

—MIKE MURDOCK, host of the TV program "Wisdom Keys"

You have the ability to accomplish so much by making a slight change in your routine. Leave time, leave space, to grow. Now. Now! Not tomorrow!

—OG MANDINO, author and motivational speaker

ALL RIGHT, THEN! By now, you have likely experienced the benefits of tapping into WBC and using it to guide your decisions and facilitate the actualization of your potential. So what does it take to see your plan through all the way to the goal line? Wholehearted dedication. This chapter will lead you through daily practices and new behaviors that will help you maintain the highest level of whole-body consciousness so you can do just that.

Routines and Rituals

First, let's talk about your day-to-day life and agree on the meaning of two very common words: *routine* and *ritual*. At first glance, it is tempting to assume that these two words point pretty much to the same thing: some kind of regimen, sequence of actions, or ceremony that a person engages in repeatedly. You might sense that a slight difference exists between the two, but if you're like most people, you haven't had the occasion to clarify exactly what that distinction is. So let me spell it out. A routine is any act or series of actions that you take on a regular basis to accomplish something, whether that be preparing for work or fixing your lunch. These are basic maintenance functions with relatively little fluff. For example, you routinely do your dishes at the end of a meal. You routinely shave after you shower in the morning and before you put on a freshly laundered shirt. You may routinely get out the clothes you intend to wear the next day before going to bed at night.

A ritual, on the other hand, can fall into two general categories: the ceremonial variety or the day-to-day variety. Ceremonial rituals, which include rites of passage, are characteristic of all cultures. Some are associated with holidays or changes of season such as dressing a turkey for Thanksgiving dinner, decorating a yuletide bush or Christmas tree, lighting a menorah, or hiding colored eggs and dancing around a Maypole in the spring. In addition to cultural rituals, we see familial rituals, fraternity rituals, and the like. For the moment, let's set these aside and focus on daily rituals. So here is the distinction I want to point out: unlike a routine, which could be defined as a mundane, mindless series of actions, *a ritual is an act with intentional focus that brings about a change in the state of your mind and body.*

Let's look at the behavior of an Olympic athlete to get a clearer sense of what this means. The gymnast stands and looks at her apparatus. Then she powders her hands with chalk and looks at the apparatus again. Next she looks at her coach. Then she steps up to the line and takes several deep breaths. Her focus is intense as she looks at the parallel bars. In her mind's eye, the crowd disappears—nothing exists for her except the moment, the bars, and her desire to win the gold. She takes one last deep breath, exhales, and raises an arm before she leaps into the air.

Every move until the moment she leaps into the air has been intentional. In fact for most Olympic athletes, almost every move from the moment of waking is intended to support the desired outcome: taking home a medal. And while your challenge in life may not be to go for the gold in the Olympic sense, if you've read this far, it is likely that you are a person who won't be satisfied unless you play to the fullest.

So here is my challenge and invitation to you. Make whole-body consciousness a daily *ritual*—not just a routine. Like working a muscle, your BQ gets stronger when you use it, so don't wait for the inevitable urgency to engage this higher state of awareness. Start your day with it now.

BQ for Breakfast

Many clients who have children to get off to school, pets to feed, and other morning chores tell me that adding ten

minutes to the morning busyness is impossible. I can empathize, as I've been there myself, but I still encourage you to wake up earlier or do whatever it takes to add one ten-minute ritual—a body-mind tune-up—to your life each day. Before you even get out of bed in the morning, take

a moment to revel in whole-body consciousness and anchor yourself in that dimension of personal focus and clarity. Doing so will help you embody, maintain, and accelerate the insights and techniques you learned in the previous chapters.

This ten-minute daily ritual is the key factor for getting out and *staying out* of your head. Believe me, I am speaking from experience, not theory! Before making this my daily practice, I often woke up in the morning and immediately began drifting in whatever direction my mind would take me. The undisciplined mind loves to think about the past and the future and inevitably gets tangled up in a web of spin. When I created the ritual I am about to share with you, I found that it allowed me to stay anchored in purpose instead of spin, to remain clear about my priorities, and—most of all—to be tangibly aware of my mind, body, and spirit working together as one.

This simple ten-minute ritual is also an excellent way to prepare for any important event, from a business meeting to a hot date. It wakes up and harmonizes the body, mind, and spirit through breath, movement, visualization, and sound. It literally moves you into a more coherent IQ-BQ state and helps you forge a conscious connection between your heart, brain, gut, and spirit. It helps you access well-being, clarity, and confidence; your mind and body quiet down, and you experience a unique state of awareness.

When I do the WBC practice for breakfast, my mood and energy get turbocharged. On the other hand, on days when I skip this ritual, I tend to be more easily stressed and less sure-handed throughout the day. For instance, I may answer the phone and say or promise things I later regret. It *is* important to start the day with a healthy breakfast; so make sure BQ is on the menu!

Read through the following instructions and try it for yourself. You can do it in bed or use a mat on the floor. If you're in bed, you'll need to remove the covers. Try to make it part of your routine to begin this exercise as soon as you wake up in the morning.

1. Breathe—tune in to your belly. Take five slow, deep whole-body belly breaths, inhaling and exhaling out of your mouth. Fill your belly, then relax your jaw and throat, and sigh aloud on the exhalation. Touch your belly with your hands.

Visualize sending energy from the top of your chest down to the bottom of your belly, and imagine filling your belly as though it were a beach ball. Hold your breath and imagine moving the beach ball from the base of your pelvis up toward your throat. Move the ball up and down several times until you feel a need to exhale, and let out an audible sigh as you do. Repeat this three times to expand your diaphragm. Do three more full, deep breaths, and visualize the oxygen traveling throughout your entire body. If you like, try an affirmation such as *I am sending oxygen to my neck area*, or *I send oxygen to my entire body from head to toe.*

2. Move. Put your heels flat on your bed or the floor and bring your knees up, sliding your heels closer to your bottom. As you breathe, tilt your pelvis forward and arch your back on the in-breath, then move your pelvis back down as your back flattens out on the exhale. Do this five times. Notice your spine waking up and your body filling with energy.

3. Appreciate. Say a blessing or express appreciation for the spiritual dimension of your existence. This could be a prayer or a simple expression of gratitude, such as "I am thankful for another day." Take five more whole-body breaths and anchor this grateful attitude in your body and mind.

4. Scan and declare. Remember to continue breathing fully, scanning your body for any of the following:

- Is your breath smooth or choppy?
- Is your breath moving from the bottom of your belly to the top of your chest?
- Is your body changing temperature as you breathe?
- Is anything in your body moving or shaking nervously?
- Is your heart beating fast or slow?
- Is there any place that feels pain, tightness, or special sensation?
- Are you feeling any emotions, light or strong?

Listen to what your body is telling you.

Once you are in contact with your body sensations and feelings, declare them out loud or silently. You can do all of them at once or one at a time. For example, "I am noticing that my breath is short, my jaw is clenched, and I am worried," or "My leg is shaking nervously," or "I feel excited."

Follow your instincts and let your body prompt you. You can continue to lie down, or you can sit or stand up if you feel moved to at this time. I like to move uncomfortable feelings by shaking my whole body; this can be done either standing or lying down. Breathe in and out through your nose or mouth and shake your body. Then rest.

5. Praise—tune in to your heart. Thank your body and love it exactly as it is. Talk to it and give it conscious permission to relax. Attend to any parts that are nervous or tight, and send love especially to areas of your body that you have felt unhappy with or embarrassed about. Give your body positive affirmations, such as "I love my shoulders and appreciate all that they have carried for me. I now release them and see them relaxed and happy." Give those body parts even more love with touch and massage.

6. Remember—connect with your life purpose. Continue breathing consciously, and remember your life purpose. Say it to yourself a couple of times, and notice how it feels in your body. Include that in your declaration too. For example: *My life purpose is to help children learn more about the world they live in. I notice that I smile and my belly feels warm as I say that.*

7. Visualize—tune in to your mind's eye. See yourself moving through the day fully connected to your whole body. Set an intention for how you want your day to unfold, breathing calmly in and out through your nose. Should disturbing thoughts arise, breathe out rapidly several times through your mouth. Do this until your mind quiets, then breathe slowly again through your nose. See yourself having a miraculous day, exactly the way you want it to be. Now you are ready for your day.

Power Moves: Ritualize Tapping into WBC

An international ad agency conducted a global study to get data on the how, what, and when of the daily regimes in which all humans engage. They found that while many of these habitual behaviors are ingrained patterns with no emotion attached to them, others clearly brought about a transformation by moving the person from one emotional state to another. In an article for *Business Week*, Diane Brady reports that the research revealed five distinct transitional categories: "preparing for battle" (the morning ritual); "feasting" (reconnecting with your tribe over food); "sexing up" (primping); "returning to camp" (leaving the workplace); and "protecting yourself for the future" (the ritual before bed). Daily rituals "make things visible," says anthropologist Victor Turner, who studied the Ndembu tribe in Africa. Turner points out that the Ndembu word for ritual symbols is derived from the same root as the word used to designate markers on a trail. Seen in this way, your daily rituals can point the way and prevent you from losing sight of your goals.

Equally important as beginning your day with WBC is developing your ability to return or reestablish yourself in WBC throughout the day. The three WBC "power moves" I share below will allow you to rewire your body-mind over time. These power moves will sound familiar; they are nutshell versions of the skills you focused on in earlier chapters. Read them as a review and summary of the work you have done up until now. Then begin to practice them regularly until they become second nature to you. This is part of your daily maintenance.

Each of the power moves begins with an affirmation that serves as a reminder and formal starting point. You can also invent your own bodily cues or gestures to anchor each power move in your awareness. Use these regularly, and you will establish a deep neurological groove that affords you the ability to flow toward calm in the midst of any storm.

Power Move 1: Disengage

You can consciously step back and disengage from any situation that rattles your cage with this simple move. In order to live a balanced life, it is crucial that you learn to recognize when you've entered into a spin trap and have a strategy that allows you to instantly escape and step into the whole-body consciousness where you are *at choice* rather than *in reaction*. Buddhist teachings point to the fact that a neutral state of relaxed awareness known as *enlightenment* is your intrinsic nature. This state is always there; it's like a backdrop that never changes, no matter what the day has in store for you in the foreground.

Power Move 1 is designed to give you access to this expansive state of awareness in a snap. It begins with an affirmation that shifts your focus inward. You might anchor this power move with a simple gesture, like tapping yourself on the forehead between your eyebrows. Then, you simply practice breathing deeply like you have throughout this book to quiet the mind, relax, and bring your awareness to your body. This simple process brings you fully into the present, where whole-body consciousness is readily available. This limits stress and prevents escalation of any conflict—be it internal or external.

The affirmation for Power Move 1 is, *In this moment, I choose to be fully present in my mind **and** body.* Repeat this affirmation several times to initiate the state of WBC.

The next step of Power Move 1 is deep belly breathing. This allows you to be present, relaxed, and connected to mind and body at the same time. Breathing deep into your belly calms the nervous system and soothes the flight-or-fight reaction. Making decisions in flight-or-fight mode can be dicey; better to step back when intensity strikes and find a relaxed, calm state before reacting in a way that adds fuel to the fire.

Most of us are "chest breathers" who utilize only the upper third of our lungs. Master yoga teacher and author Donna Farhi explains the detrimental effect of this: "When we breathe in our chest, we are using our secondary or accessory respiratory muscles instead of primary muscles. Relying on these weak upper-body muscles develops chronic tension in the back, shoulders, and neck. Chest breathing creates a chronic state of anxiety." Focused breathing techniques relax the body and change your state of consciousness. Your subjective experience of a situation becomes more objective; your behavior is more reality-based, your course of action more effective, and your outcomes more aligned with your values and goals.

In this calm, neutral state, you are ready to engage Power Move 2.

Power Move 2: Gather Information,
Separate Fact from Fiction

This move allows you to view your situation more objec-
tively and separate facts from spin thoughts. The affirmation
for Power Move 2, which you will also repeat several times,
is, *I now choose to gather accurate information and evaluate it with
both my mind and body.* You might decide to anchor this power
move in your body with a simple gesture, like bringing your
hands together with interlocked fingers and placing them
over your heart. It's less important what gesture you use, and
more important that you choose one to ritualize the shift from
uncertainty to clarity.

Many decision-making systems recommend looking at a
list of positives and negatives, or costs and payoffs, in any given
situation. This approach would have you figure out which
choice is best from a largely rational point of view, which
doesn't necessarily change your state. Power Move 2 engages
IQ *and* BQ, mind *and* body, and facts *and* feelings as parts of the
decision-making process. You learn how to scan your body-
mind with awareness, using WBC to witness and consciously
recognize your thoughts, physical sensations, and emotions.
Once you inquire into and articulate (aloud or silently) the
self-evident truths that you discover in any given moment, you
can respond appropriately to what is happening.

Use Power Move 2 to sort out circumstantial evidence and
separate facts from false assumptions based on your fears or
outdated beliefs. This perspective helps you recognize and
accept what you cannot control and focus on what you can
control—and get creative.

Power Move 2 operates on the principle that what we
become conscious of in WBC no longer controls us. This

awareness allows us to see *and* feel where we are operating at cross-purposes and to understand how this creates unnecessary stress and conflict. You can learn to regularly use Power Move 2 when you fall into old habits of thinking and thus recover your confidence and purpose. Get out of your head and into WBC, and you are ready to take action on your *real* desires in Power Move 3.

Power Move 3: Make a Clear Decision and Carry It Through

The affirmation for Power Move 3 is, *I can make a powerful choice and follow through on my decision.* You will repeat this several times at the start of this move.

While the first two power moves are designed to help you attain a calm, balanced state in which you feel inwardly alert and clear-eyed as to what *is,* instead of what is *imagined,* the third power move allows you to focus your personal power in alignment with your deepest desire—your passion and your purpose—and then bring that power fully into the decision-making process.

This move is all about getting clear, from a place of inner assuredness and power, on what you *truly* want in any situation, knowing your desire is essential so that you can choose and act decisively. We access this clarity of intention and desire in Power Move 3 based on the information we accessed in the first two moves. When you are aligned with your overall desired outcome, the power of that larger purpose enhances the decision-making process.

Weave these power moves into your life, and you will gain a wider, more deeply informed perspective on situations that might once have baffled you. In time, they will become your natural way of moving through life.

SET Spot Checks to Keep You Connected

So let's check up on your new ability to return to or reestablish yourself in WBC throughout the day. During my private intensives, I ask my clients every few hours, "What's your self-evident truth right now?" "What's your body telling you?" People are often amazed to recognize the pervasive tendency to drift away from their body and get frozen in thought. A SET spot check is a simple, state-shifting "whole-body scan" that can be done in five to thirty seconds and that integrates and realigns mind, body, breath, and emotions and brings us back to a place of choice, awareness, and power in the moment. Several times during the day, take a time-out and ask yourself, "What is my self-evident truth?" *Just remembering to ask yourself that one question several times a day will greatly improve your life.* Take a few moments and notice your body. Notice any tension, any relaxation, anywhere. Are your shoulders relaxed? Tense? Are your hands gripping too tightly? Are you breathing in a relaxed, natural fashion? Is your posture comfortable? Make any adjustments that will make you feel better. You just did a quick version of the self-evident truth process, an SET spot check.

As with most worthy endeavors, staying out of your head and boosting your BQ requires regular attention and discipline. The daily ritual, power moves, and SET spot checks will yield the best results when you do them regularly. Maintaining the state of whole-body consciousness prepares you to respond calmly, clearly, and confidently in any situation. It also opens the door to all kinds of miraculous events and discoveries, as you will see in the next chapter when I share the remarkable adventure WBC took me on when I traveled to India and put it to the ultimate test.

≋ 12 ≋

A Day in the Life of Whole-Body Consciousness

Impossible situations can become possible miracles.

—REVEREND ROBERT H. SCHULLER

≋ Northern California, 1996 ≋
A Foggy November Morning

WAKE UP FEELING tight. Overnight, my body seems to have morphed into one massive ache. Before my eyes even get a chance to focus, my mind is off and running, spinning wild tales. *I must be having a heart attack.* One nightmare scenario after another comes to mind. I fight the urge to bury the feelings swirling around inside me and remind myself to breathe and feel. After a few conscious breaths, I notice that my throat is constricted. I feel as if someone has placed a hundred-pound dumbbell across my chest. I go right into my head, and the voice of panic says, *I must be dying.* I catch myself, switch gears, and practice what I preach by declaring out loud, "I notice choking feelings in my throat and a feeling of being crushed across my chest." I press my fingertips onto my throat and chest as I take a few more deep breaths. My throat and chest continue to tighten, and then I suddenly yell, "Get off my chest! Let me go!"

Wondering what this trapped feeling could possibly be, I tune in to my body more deeply and repeat, "Get off! Let me go! Let me go!" I keep breathing deeply and repeat this several times, then begin to push my hands out in front of me. I close my eyes, and my bedroom disappears. Suddenly, I am nine years old on my parents' front lawn in Baltimore, and one of the older guys in the neighborhood is sitting on my chest.

I roar, "Let me go!" over and over, breathing fully, moving my chest, and flailing my arms. I visualize pushing him off of me, as relief floods through my body. I open my eyes and look around my bedroom. I reflect on what has just happened. My anger and fear has been buried for a long time. The emotional memory of that incident mirrors the powerlessness I am feeling in my life at the moment. I remind myself that I am not the powerless child I was when the older boy was holding me down on my front lawn, and I feel a wave of calm flow through me. My breath begins to flow easily. I have a "straight talk" with myself and sort out what is real and what is not.

Nothing I was thinking is true. I am not having a heart attack. I begin to wonder if this experience is telling me something I need to know. I sit quietly for a while and listen to my body. I relax and revel in whole-body consciousness. My mind lets go, and I feel an exhilarating freedom I haven't felt for months. *I want more of this*, I think, half aloud. *Lots more.* Moments later, I get a strong inner nudge to *just do it*—take some time off and properly rethink my life. It occurs to me that the farther away from Marin County I can get, the more clearly I'll be able to see what's really happening in my world. I take a breath in anticipation of getting some direction on where to go. I close my eyes, and after several long moments, a distinct image comes into focus. My heartbeat quickens as villages, temples, and the Ganges River appear in my mind's eye. I take a deep breath and feel a very strong instinct to travel to India. *Odd*, I think. *India is the last place on Earth I want to visit.*

The India Odyssey

I drive into San Francisco the next day to check out the Indian Embassy—just to "feel out" this sudden, inexplicable urge and look into a travel visa. As I enter the building, I'm instantly overwhelmed with fear. I go into my head and dis-connect from my body. Frozen in my mind and numb in my body, I look around at the photos on the wall. India begins to seem like a bad idea. Still, I get in line for my visa. My mind is spinning with fear; my thoughts are scrambling: *I might get malaria or dysentery. It's too polluted. I won't be able to take seeing the poverty. I won't be safe.* I leave the visa line and quickly walk outside to sit in my car. I am too uncomfortable in my skin to think clearly, so I decide to go home and forget the whole idea. That night, my mind and body play out a tug-of-war. I go back and forth between moments of whole-body con-sciousness that feel incredibly exciting and are accompanied by a gut sense that a trip to India will give me exactly what I need right now and hours of agony as horrific what-ifs play in my mind.

After hours of fixating on the terrible thoughts, I decide to move some energy in my body and change my consciousness. I get out of bed and begin jumping on my mini-trampoline. Ahhh, I start to breathe deeply, feeling some connection to my body again. As I continue to move, breathe, and feel my body sensations, I realize that nothing that my mind cooked up was real. I return to the Indian Embassy the next day, grounded in my body and excited. I secure my visa.

What Am I Doing Here?

One week and a seemingly endless flight later, I arrive in Bombay. I notice a booth advertising an air-conditioned bus ride to a wonderful city with temples. I purchase a ticket. A man leads me to the bus five blocks away. I board the bus, which has no air-conditioning, and watch as four men struggle to turn a crank in the front of the vehicle to get it started. My mind says, "I got ripped off, where will I be taken?" But my body instinct encourages me to trust and keep going. Five hours later, I find myself in the middle of a wild, crowded street scene. I close my eyes for one long, deep breath and ask myself, *What am I doing here*?

As I open my eyes, I feel very present and alive. I look around and see homes made of cardboard, people huddled around fires cooking, a wedding procession parading down the street with drummers and candle bearers, bicyclists and scooter drivers dodging and honking at each other, and a man urinating. I've visited many parts of the world, but this is unlike anything I've ever encountered. Here, life is inside-out: everything is happening on the street rather than behind walls. As I watch the people who are so at ease in this unruly environment, I feel like a fully clothed person in a nudist camp.

I start to laugh, and my body relaxes a little. I remember a comic book called *What Am I Doing Here?* that I owned as a young boy. The book featured a skinny guy in a turban and loincloth, asking himself this crucial question in the midst of all sorts of chaos. I remember a scene involving a bullfight, another one involving a mob, and a third in which he's alone on a mountaintop. As a kid, that book fascinated me and left a deep impression on my psyche. I hadn't thought about it for over forty years. Now, *I* am the one appearing on the page, wondering what I am doing in India. I breathe deeply and take in my surroundings again.

Then it hits me: *I am in India, on my own, and something marvelous is about to happen that could completely change my life. That is what I asked for, and that is why I'm here.*

Cow Consciousness

My thoughts give way, and I notice a large herd of cows ambling down the street, right in the midst of the wedding procession. The cows look relaxed and content, as if they belong exactly where they are—smack in the middle of everything. No one is concerned or put off by their presence. As I watch this oddity, I begin to relax and notice a calm feeling flowing through my body. I wonder, *How would life be if I were as certain of my place in the scheme of things as those cows?* In that moment, my journey takes on new dimension and meaning. India is the ultimate test of whole-body consciousness. I tune in to the cows and absorb their way of being—they are simply *here*, gently inhab-

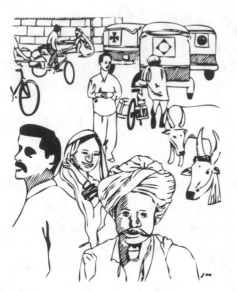

iting their wide bodies. I laugh out loud at the radical new philosophy India has offered me— *cow consciousness!*

"Cow consciousness!" The more I say it, the more I like it. I am still aware of the chaos outside, yet I feel content and serene. The chatter in my mind is gone. I feel present and alive, aware of my whole body from head to toe. I had stumbled out of my head and into the world.

An Impromptu Meeting with the Dalai Lama

The next day India awakens me early with her pungent smells and cackling chickens. I am filled with anticipation as I emerge from my room onto the street. I practice cow consciousness and start walking wherever my body instinctively wants to go. I nod and smile and mutter "namaste" to the curious, turbaned Sikhs and children who follow me along an alleyway. I chuckle to myself thinking *namaste* sounds like "no mistakes," and think up a new word, "namastakes." (By now you are getting an idea of how I entertain myself!) As I notice my body walking down the alley and the people still following me, my mind starts again asking, *What am I doing here? Why did I choose to walk down this alley? Am I in danger?* I remember my commitment and connect to my whole-body consciousness and know the answer to my question. I am following my instincts, having mind–body conversations, and trusting that I am in the perfect place at the perfect time. I say to myself, "Namastakes!"

I realize that my recent waking up in fear that I was dying from a heart attack, the internal experience of pushing my neighbor off my chest, and choosing to come to India are all important steps in my life journey. I assure myself that there are indeed no mistakes and that I am walking down this alley right now for some perfect reason. I move forward, following my body instincts. As I continue walking, I see a man standing under a sign that says "Tibetan Medicine." He gestures to me, and I walk toward him without question. He invites me to walk up several flights of stairs into a small office. Another man stands as I enter and says two words: "Dalai Lama." I shrug and repeat, "Dalai Lama?" He nods and says, "Come." He turns and walks back down the stairs. I check in with my body and follow him wordlessly, honoring the sense that this is exactly what I should be doing. Still having my body–mind conversation, I remember to breathe and tune in to my feelings, opening myself in trust to whatever is next. He mounts a scooter and motions for me to climb on the back. I do, feeling my excitement growing as we drive through a maze of busy streets into the tree–filled countryside. The smells change; the air cools. I feel exhilarated. We arrive in a large field, where a small circle of colorfully robed Tibetan monks are gathered. One of the monks looks straight at me as I climb off the scooter and walk toward them. He greets me with laughter (he is often affectionately called "the Jolly Lama") and warmth, as if to say "Nice to see you again."

I am ecstatic; he *is* the Dalai Lama! Namastakes!

If someone had asked me a week ago, "If you could meet with anyone in the world to get some clarity and be relieved of your inner struggle, who would it be?" I would have said "the Dalai Lama" without hesitation. I had come to respect him as

one of our greatest living teachers but had not even thought of looking for him on this journey.

We are motioned to sit. The Dalai Lama speaks about kindness. He reminds us to have compassion for ourselves and for others, to relax and trust. His message is exactly what I need to hear. My heart is soothed, and I feel inspired. My passion for life is back!

During my remaining miracle-filled weeks in India, I am pleased to abide in cow consciousness much of the time. Many of the old emotional wounds and scary thoughts I had been carrying in my body were released.

Udder Happiness

I returned to California with many gifts of understanding and, most of all, confirmation that the guidance of my brilliant body would take me wherever I needed to go.

My friends, I highly encourage you to trust your innate body-based intelligence. Take action based on the wisdom of your whole body, not just your mind. Choose your actions by sensing and feeling, trusting that your brilliant body can take you where you want to go, even if you don't know where that is yet. Get out of your head as much as possible and stay there grounded in whole-body consciousness . . . and enjoy the ride!

INDEX

About the Author

S TEVE SISGOLD IS many things to many people—as an author, speaker, entertainer, body-centered coach, and businessman, he has modeled and taught thousands how to use their innate body intelligence to create better health, prosperity, and richer and more authentic relationships.

Steve owned a successful advertising and PR firm, was number one of five hundred salespeople with a major corporation, and is a breakthrough coach to bestselling self-help authors, Grammy Award–winning recording artists, as well as business leaders and holistic practitioners. He holds a master's in communications, a BS in business, and certifications in body-centered psychotherapy and relationship counseling.

Steve is available for speaking engagements and group trainings.

Other Offerings from Steve Sisgold: Transformational Products to Enhance Your Life

Audio CD:
Infinite Possibilities
Designed to use daily for meditation and conscious manifesting, this CD takes you on the life's-purpose journey presented in Chapter 7 of this book. The music behind Steve's voice was

composed by internationally acclaimed recording artist James Asher.

Four digital downloads:
Boost Your Power of Attraction
Unlike any audio program on the market, this lively, interactive, and very informative recording helps you use all of your innate intelligence to proactively improve your personal and business life.
Discovering and Embodying Your Life's Purpose
Take a journey into the most important aspect of your life, your life's purpose. This audio product gives you inspiration, inner wisdom, and focus.
Reduce Stress, Produce More
This audio product will help you or someone you care about cope with the stresses of life changes. Steve's unique style and user-friendly techniques provide practical skills for stress reduction.
Triumph over Trauma
A new breakthrough film documentary produced by Steve and Gay Hendricks. The story of this riveting, life-changing journey (described in Chapter 6) filmed in Poland and Germany appeared in thirty-three magazines.

To contact Steve, receive his free e-letter, get information on tranformational retreats, or order or download these products:

www.whatsyourbodytellingyou.com
www.stevesisgold.com
Phone: 415-302-5922
E-mail: steves@onedream.com